to Dr. H

Thank

for all the years you have

effectively been my doctor.

FOR THIS I WAS CREATED

Purposeful Living

BY

RUTH LAURA JONES THOMAS

May my story be an
Inspiration to you as it
has been to me!
            Lovingly,
            Ruth L. Thomas

CONTENTS

ACKNOWLEDGEMENTS

This story of my life would never have been written if my youngest son, Daran, had not started me on this journey back in the year 2000. It began when he started asking questions about my life. My answers to his questions developed into about 20 pages of emails. This became the basis for actually writing this story 10 years later.

Of the many people deserving thanks for their role in the production of this book, I would like to start with my faithful husband who encouraged me, read and re-read my manuscripts through many endless days, weeks, months, and years, and who gave me guidance, correction, and editing of our life's story. Without his support, I'm sure this would never have been finished.

But there are also many others I must thank as well, starting with my dear father (though unknown to him, as he has been in Glory with the Lord since 1996), who poured into me life-giving teachings in God's Word. He, along with my mother, dedicated me when I was born to the Lord that if the Lord would so will, I would become a missionary.

This faith of my father goes back through many generations of faithful followers of Jesus Christ, the Savior of the World.

I have a great heritage.

Many others who have mentored me throughout my spiritual journey are professor Dr. Virgil Olson at Bethel College; Nancy Anderson, a fellow missionary; and countless books and taped sermons from Joy Dawson of YWAM. But most of all I have received so much healing and freedom in our wonderful church, the Inland Vineyard Church in Corona, CA, with pastor Travis Twyman. Without his faithful, anointed teachings and the love, support, and encouragement of the church family, I could not have completed this manuscript.

Then there are those who took the time to read at least some of my stories and give me suggestions: Dr. Deborah Thomas-Jones, my youngest child; Aunt Elnora Jones Emmons, my cousins Janis and Jeanette; my dear spiritual daughters, Candy and Cory; and finally my editor, Nate Prior, who laboriously edited every word and sentence of this manuscript, and without whom you would be reading my hen scratches.

Glenn M. Jones   Gladys Williams Jones

IN HONOR OF

My Father, Glenn Merton Jones,
who was there to guide me through my difficult years.
Without him I may not have found a joyful and fulfilling life.

DEDICATED TO

My pride and joy: Kevin, Denise, David, Daran, and Debi. And my grandchildren: Brittney and Tony, Ian and Jacqueline, Dominique, Mia and Zoe. In the hope that the legacy God has given you will live on in

January 2012

generations to come.

4

FOR THIS I WAS CREATED

PROLOGUE

I believe I have lived a long and meaningful life. I have traveled the world and in partnership with my husband Fred, we have raised five beautiful children who have given us six adorable grandchildren (at this writing).

I had the privilege of tasting what it would be like to be a classical pianist in my early years and have known the excitement of playing for large audiences and receiving awards. I also know what it is like to spend years in another country helping the poor and seeing God work in wondrous ways in the lives of countless people.

I also have known depression, deep loss, feelings of inadequacy, unworthiness, and an emotional break-down; then to see God lift me out of these pits and restore my life again to wholeness and happiness. God has definitely been with me through thick and thin.

Looking back I have always wondered for what purpose I was created? I have come to understand that each person is put on this earth with a special gift from God. That, if they find it and live out of this passion, then they will find true joy, peace, love, and fulfillment. I believe I have discovered that gift: I am so passionate about seeing God at work in my life and in other people's lives. I feel that my gift is watching what God is doing around me and finding ways to join Him in what He is doing...

This happens in many ways:

One of my favorite ways is when I travel. Before I fly anywhere I always ask God to sit me next to people that He may want to encourage toward Him. Sometimes He does and sometimes he just wants me to read or rest.

A recent experience I had was when I was flying home from a two-week trip to see my three children and one grandchild who live far from me. As I was waiting to be called for my flight a gentleman, about my age, came by and asked if he could sit in the empty seat next to me. I found out he had retired a few years earlier as a Geology professor from the University of Minnesota -- the same school where I got my degree in Elementary Education! He was a writer and somehow connected to the UN. We talked about the Darfur trauma and other issues. Then we got around to discussing religion. I was so blessed by this encounter and could see he was searching for God. Our flight was called and our conversation ended abruptly, but I walked away amazed at God's goodness in allowing me to have this encounter!

Another time God allowed me to sit next to a Muslim lady (One of the only Muslims on a large plane). We were seated in a row with three seats; I was by the window, the mother was in the middle, and a very large man was next to her. Her daughter, whom she kept trying to communicate with, was across the aisle. I prayed, "Lord, show me how I can show love to these ladies". Immediately I saw something I could do: I asked the gentleman if he would be willing to trade seats with the daughter. When the mother saw what I did, she was so grateful that she hugged and kissed me! Then we began talking. I mostly listened as she and her daughter berated this terribly sinful American culture, but eventually I got to share with her about God's love and Isa (Jesus). Again this blessed me immensely for days afterward! Just to be one little "spoke in a wheel" working with the Holy Spirit to encourage people on their spiritual journey toward the one true God is so rewarding. The things of this world hold little interest to me. I have found the true and living God and I am passionate about others having the opportunity to know Him too.

The following chapters are my story, and Fred's, and our story together. It is written to leave a legacy to our children and to upcoming generations of the Goodness and Greatness of God Almighty -- The Maker of all things both great and small. And it is written to honor His Son, Jesus Christ, who sacrificed His life so we might be given new life in Him, thus fulfilling our destiny. My prayer is: *"Let our children see your glory at work"* (Psalm 90:16b) through the pages of God's story played out in our lives.

This could be a book about all our failures as parents, mentors, and spouses, but I know that to rehearse all our failures does not produce fruit. So I have chosen to write my memoirs about how God has taken our failures and brought us through by changing our characters to be more like Jesus -- that is our hearts' desire.

I join King David in his prayer when he said in Psalm 71:18: *"Let me proclaim your power to this new generation, your mighty miracles to all those who come after me."* May all who read these pages be blessed and encouraged as they seek and find, as we did, true happiness and fulfillment in this life as well as in the life to come.

50th Wedding Anniversary

Chapter 1

ETERNAL AND IMMORTAL

We had just finished a youth meeting in our home in Manila in 1983. As we opened the door for people to leave, our cute little black Dachshund dashed outside into the darkness. Fred ran after the little rascal. Across the street in a parked car, the driver was talking to the security guard of the stately house behind him.

Fred thought our dog, Tommie, might have run in the bushes in front of the car, so he went over there looking for him. Suddenly the driver shouted, "What do you want? What are you looking for?" Fred answered, "I'm looking for my dog". The driver got out of his car and provoked Fred by knocking off his glasses. When Fred reached down to pick them up, the driver lifted his arm and shot his 9mm Sterling revolver into the air twice, shouting, "I kill you! I kill you!"

You have heard some Christians say that at such times they sense God-given peace, calm and comfort. At this moment Fred did not have this feeling! But, just then, Tommie came running by proving Fred was not lying. As he headed toward our house wondering if he would be shot in the back, the assailant again shouted, "Go home, Americano!"

Fred soon came into the house looking quite shaken. He realized once again that the old adage is really true: "Under God's Almighty love and care nothing can touch us; we are immortal until we die, then we are eternal."

A few years later, in 1989, there was an attempted military coup d'état in Manila. At this time Fred was an Associate Pastor of the Union Church of Manila (UCM). We lived in the subdivision of Green

Hills—about 15 miles from the church. Our house sat in the middle of the "war zone". We were somewhat protected as we were inside a gated community of about 200 homes with walls about 30 feet high surrounding this complex.

It was decided on the fourth day of the coup, which was Sunday, that the worshippers from UCM should try to gather together in neighborhoods instead of risking coming to the church. Our home was designated as a worship center. Only three families showed up, but a fourth came just as we were closing the service. They had packed up their personal belongings in their car with their children and stopped to tell us they were headed for a "safe house" hotel designated by the US Embassy—away from the war zone. Earlier a small missile had landed in their front yard—just a little too close for comfort.

After they left the rest of us talked about what we should do. There were rumors that the opposition would come into our subdivision and take over our homes as a base for taking over the government.

One of the families, an Australian couple there on business, suggested we pack up with our two daughters, Debi and Denise, and go to their house until the "war" was over. All six of us piled into our car and headed toward the front gate. When the guard finally got the gate open, we saw to our right that the fighting was going on only a block away and heading our way. Just then a stray bullet grazed the arm of a soldier near our car. He was immediately put on a TV flat bed truck that was parked across the street covering the action of the "war". We quickly turned left and headed for our friend's house. That evening the opposition surrendered. As we drove home we saw about 4,000 of the rebel troops in the parking lot of the shopping area in front of our subdivision sitting on the ground with soldiers guarding them.

These are just a couple of many experiences we had seeing the protection of God in the 32 years we spent in the Philippines telling the Good News that Jesus is the sacrificial Lamb and long-awaited Messiah who has come to live and die for those who accept Him into their hearts. The following chapters will unfold to the reader the "Great Things God has done".

9

Chapter 2
(1934-1952)

MY EARLY LIFE
Ruth's Story

"I am fearfully and wonderfully made...in the image of God"
Psalm 139:14

I came out of the womb bubbling over with creativity, curiosity and great potential despite challenging beginnings. I had a great ancestry; my mother came from Scottish and English descent and my father from Welsh and English ancestry (more can be read about this great heritage in the Appendix).

In 1934, the country was still recovering from the Great Depression of 1929. When I was born my father was picking up potatoes for $1.00 a day. We lived in a two room upstairs apartment, across the street from my father's parents and my 13-year-old aunt Alnora.

I am so thankful for Christian parents who desired God's best for me. One Sunday after church they brought me to the altar where they dedicated me to the Lord. They believed, as I do, in partnering with God to "bring up a child in the way she should go," and that God would send a guardian angel to watch over their little one. I remember my father telling me years later, when I was about to leave for the Philippines as a missionary, that at my dedication he asked the Lord to call me to be a missionary. This was something he really wanted to do himself, but God had other plans for his life.

I was struck with many illnesses in my childhood. I had pneumonia, whooping cough, and other sicknesses within my first two years of life. Dad said one time he ran blocks to the doctor, with me in his arms, because I was so sick he thought I would die.

Another time when my father sent my mother to camp for a week of rest, my aunt Alnora took care of me as she also often babysat me. "You cried a lot," she says. "I guess you missed your mommy." At age 91, she is still my hero!

God was really watching out for our family, which he does for those who follow Him. Dad had been taking a drafting course by correspondence, so he decided to try to get a job in that field. He read in the newspaper that there were two openings in a company in Lansing, Michigan 60 miles away. He hitchhiked to the company and applied. What were his chances with 200 men who had also applied waiting to get one of these jobs? After hours of waiting, the CEO of the company finally came in the door and called out, "Can anyone here do a specific kind of drafting?" Dad immediately shouted, "I can." (Actually he had never heard of it!) But he was hired, and the head of the project took pity on him and taught him how to do the job. This job only lasted a few months, but it was enough to support his little family at such a desperate time. Each weekend he would hitchhike home to see his wife and baby.

While Dad was busy making a living for his family, I was learning to explore the world around me. Grandma Nora's homemade bread, warm from the oven and covered with butter and sugar, was my invitation to visit her. So at barely two years old I would toddle over to ask grandma for this very tasty morsel, but this great pleasure soon ended when Dad got a job in Detroit working for Vickers, Inc. He moved his little family to an apartment near his office and worked there until he was 62 years old.

Dad worked his way up to Assistant Chief Engineer and at one time had 40 men working under him in his design engineering department. But when his company sold out to Sperry-Rand, he was demoted. Eventually he was given an early retirement with a year's salary. I am certain that this was very hard on him. Earlier during World War II he was very valuable in the area of hydraulics. I remember him telling me about a problem he had designing the hydraulics for dropping bombs. He prayed much about this; suddenly, one night he awoke with the answer and the problem was solved.

The Company also used him as a "trouble-shooter" and would send him all over the States to solve problems. One time he and a co-worker were sent out to correct a problem in Kansas. When they got to the airport to return home, they discovered that there was only one seat left on the plane and Dad thought it best that his friend get home to

his family, and he could wait until the next day. Sadly, that plane crashed! What Dad intended for good turned out to be evil. I can remember how much he suffered with guilt.

When I was almost four years old my brother, Wesley Merton, was born. While my mother was in the hospital having Wesley, whom we nicknamed Bud, I became very ill with Scarlet fever; I had to be quarantined and a nurse, Vera Smith, came to take care of me. Dad had to sleep in the basement and Mom couldn't come home with the new baby until I was well.

Ruth & Gladys (mom)

Soon after the baby came home, I was given a baby doll with a stuffed body that could even take a bottle, probably to help me have my own "baby" now that a new baby was in the home. I was a very curious child and loved to discover how things worked. One day, I decided to see if my baby could eat solid food, so I began stuffing baby food into her open mouth. My mother didn't discover this until a very strong odor led her to find out the truth. To my sadness, she had to throw my doll away. That was when I became very jealous of baby Bud, and one day I pushed him off the bed when my mother wasn't looking.

It is amazing Bud survived; I was always using him as my guinea pig while trying to satisfy my curiosity. On one occasion, at the age of six, I took my then 2-year-old brother to visit my friend who lived on the third floor of an apartment building nearby our rented house. We had to climb three flights of stairs on the outside of the building where she lived. When we finally got to the top, I noticed the electric wires attached to the poles just above us and was curious to know what would happen if we touched one. Little Bud became my guinea pig. I lifted him up as high as I could trying about three times, but he lacked a few inches of being able to touch the wires, by which we both would have been electrocuted.   Thank God for Guardian Angels!

It was soon after this that my parents saved enough money to buy a brand new, 2-bedroom bungalow on Beaverland Road in Redford, MI. Dad loved the location as there was a big wooded area across the street that ran about 2 blocks with a dirt road leading to the Rogue River. Often Dad and I would enjoy some time together taking a stroll to the river. He never said much, but I just felt so loved and peaceful when I would take his hand as we walked.

I can also remember watching out the window waiting for dad to come home at night. The first thing he would do was to take Mom in his arms and give her a big kiss. I loved to watch; it made me feel so happy and secure. Somehow I knew that, even though they often had arguments, they still loved each other.

Then he would take time to play with Bud and me. Usually he would get down on the floor and we would climb on his back and get a "horsey ride". I loved Dad dearly and I longed for a physical touch from him, but hugging and kissing and telling each other "I love you" were really not a part of our family rituals.

One day after this fun time with Dad, he was sitting in his big chair reading the newspaper. I looked at him longingly. Finally, I got up enough courage to jump into his lap and hug and kiss him. This was such a strong emotional experience for me that I quickly jumped out of his lap and ran in the bedroom, flung myself on the bed, and cried and cried. My parents couldn't figure out what was wrong with me.

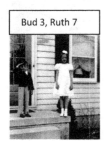
Bud 3, Ruth 7

In these early years I spent a lot of time playing with paper dolls. I was particularly fond of the Dionne Quintuplets who were exactly my age and the first in known history where all five babies survived. Mom would buy me the latest paper doll books of the Quintuplets. Sometimes I even made my own paper dolls by cutting people from catalogues and then dressing them also with designer clothes from the same catalogue .I also had about 10 dolls of various sizes. I would

13

fall asleep with them all lined up with me in bed. I loved the world of imagination and creativity.

Dad would often take Bud and me in his 1939 Plymouth up to see my grandparents on weekends. This was about 120 miles from Detroit over two-lane paved roads. It would take all day to get there. There were no freeways at that time. I again loved having this time with Dad. But one time, as we were driving along, the car door flew open and the wind almost pulled me out. Dad grabbed my dress just in time. He really saved my life. My guardian angel was again put to work.

When I was about six, Mom had an appendectomy and I went to stay at Cousin Mary Beth's house. My hair, which was usually kept in long beautiful curls, thanks to Mom, was now a snarly mess. Aunt Helene started brushing and told me, "Now hold still and don't you cry." I had a very tender scalp and soon tears were coming down my face, but I never made a peep. Mary Beth saw me crying and said, "Aw, Mom, be more gentle; she's crying." Mary Beth was always looking out for me like a big sister. I felt such a bond with her. She lived three bus rides away from where I lived, so I didn't get to see her very often.

********** Jeannie

I was a very shy child and found it hard to make friends in this new neighborhood. But in school I met a true soul mate—Jeannie; we stayed friends all of our lives. We did everything together. Her parents were Catholic and mine were Baptists, so her mother told her she could play with me, but she could not become a Baptist! Later in life she discovered the joy of having a deeper relationship with Jesus no matter what church one goes to. Today she and her three children have all experienced this Spirit-filled life with Jesus.

With Jeannie – 8th grade

Jeannie and I were inseparable. Though she lived on the other side of the woods, she would stop by my house on the way to school each day. She told me recently that she would watch my mother curl my hair with deep longing that her mother would do the same for her.

She had three sisters and, I'm sure, her mother was far too busy to do that.

We were always thinking up fun things to do. Jeannie would probably say that I would think them up and she would help me carry them out. Jeannie and I were a perfect pair; I can't remember us ever having an argument! One summer Jeannie and I got a box of matches and took them to the edge of the woods. We decided to build a little fire just for fun; however, the wind took the sparks and soon the whole woods were on fire. Someone must have called the fire department. No one ever told on us, but we learned our lesson about the danger of playing with matches.

We also spent many hours together during the summers playing cops and robbers with other kids in the neighborhood in the woods. One of the boys, Billy, liked me. In fact he liked me so much that he made me roughly carved wooden doll furniture for my dollhouse. I always wondered if he became a carpenter by trade.

I'll never forget the day when we were 11. During one of our games, I had been captured by Billy and I was trying to get away. However, unknown to me, Dad was watching us play. Then the worst thing happened: Billy kissed me! I was horrified when I looked up and saw Dad staring at me. He just said, "Ruth, go home and wash your mouth out with soap." I jumped up, scared to death, and ran home, locking myself in the bathroom. Dad never mentioned this event to me. I think he suddenly realized his little girl was growing up. He probably wondered how to keep me safe during these next few years.–

********** Christian Upbringing

My parents did their best to teach me God's ways of living. I went to church and Sunday school every week, including Wednesday nights. When at home, Dad helped me memorize Scripture. They said that at the age of 4, I could quote the 23rd Psalm while standing on my head! Every night before bedtime we would all listen to Dad read Scripture and pray. My parents never forced me to obey God, but they gave me the atmosphere I needed where I could receive or reject God's love. I can remember in my rebellious years how these Scriptures would come back to me. How true is the Scripture that says, "Thy Word have I hid in my heart so I will not sin against Thee." (Psalm 119:11)

For Christmas when I was nine, I got a yellow pup tent with a red top. We held the tent up by a clothespin clipped to a clothesline. Bud and I would play house and bring all the dolls and playthings from inside the house to make a "comfy home" in our tent. One day I decided we should have our lunch out there too. We made our fire inside the tent—where it would be "more realistic." Of course the tent caught on fire and burned everything except the little red top. I knew I would really get a heavy punishment, so Bud and I took the little red top and buried it in the sand pit nearby. I made him promise he would never tell.

Occasionally Mom would say, "Why don't you ever take your tent out anymore and play with it?" "Oh, I'm too old for that now", I would say. But Bud was waiting for the right moment to reveal the truth—it came three years later when I told on him for something he did. He blurted out, "Well, Ruthie burned the tent down." By then everyone just laughed. He never got the revenge he had hoped for.

Poor Bud! Another time I tied him to a tree; of course, I gave him lots of room to play around the yard while I went off to visit Cousin Mary Beth. I was 11 and he was 7; I was supposed to take care of him while my mother went shopping. Thank God for guardian angels!

By now it was evident to my parents that they had a big challenge ahead in raising this creative, curious, and strong-willed child. I can remember thinking hard about whether the fun thing I wanted to do was worth a spanking. Dad finally decided that this kind of discipline just wasn't working. The next time I disobeyed, how shocked I was when, instead of a spanking, I got grounded. That really worked because I loved being outside rather than inside!

********** Bible Camp

When I was 9, our family took their vacation at a neat Bible Camp. There were crafts, games, new friends, and also time to learn more about Jesus. It was there that I realized I needed a right relationship with God. I asked Jesus to forgive my sins and come into my heart. I was so happy the next day when my teacher said to my parents, "Do you know what Ruthie did yesterday in class?" Then she had me tell them! I felt such a joy in sharing this with them. A year later I was baptized in the Detroit River as a testimony to the public that I had decided to follow Jesus and to become a member of the church. I remember how happy I felt taking this step. But I had much to learn about being a follower of Jesus.

When I was 11 I got to go to Lake Ann Bible Camp with a group from church. This was a cool camp; it used to be owned by the infamous bank robber, Al Capone. His hideout back in the woods near Traverse City, Michigan, was purchased by our church group and turned into a camp. This was the first year of its existence, so all of Al's secret stairs and exit strategies were still in place. What a fun time we had exploring this famous hideout!

However, I saw something at the camp that didn't really fit with my understanding of what it meant to follow Jesus. Movies, playing cards, dancing, and wearing lipstick were just some of the things on the list of "thou shalt nots" taught in our church. But after the evening meetings at this camp, couples would take their blankets and go down to the beach and "neck" (kiss and hug). So, was this okay? Thus began my journey of trying to figure out what it meant to be a true Christian. It would take me many years to discover the answer.

At the age of 13, Dad gave me a Philips Translation of the Bible (I believe it was the first of many modern translations). That was when I began reading my Bible and learning how to follow Jesus. I learned that God was interested in our hearts being pure and loving toward Him, not just a list of do's and don'ts.

********** Mom and Dad
I believe God gave me just the parents I needed. They weren't perfect but, I believe they did the best they knew how. One of my early memories was going with Dad to skid row in Detroit when he would preach to the broken people of our society—the homeless and the alcoholics. I got to see "up close and personal" how the "other half of society lived," and I felt so very sorry for them. Perhaps God was already preparing my heart for what I would be doing with my life.

My mother did a great job of caring for our home and our personal needs, but if I misbehaved she would just threaten me with, "Just wait until your father gets home!" He is the one who would discipline me, and I'm glad he did. Someone needed to "reel me in," as I was very strong-willed and determined to have my way. When Dad wouldn't let me play "Sardines" outside at night with my friends, I would sneak in and out of my bedroom window. I can't remember ever getting caught.

One great memory I have of my mother was when she would painstakingly curl my hair.
She had to heat the curling iron on the stove for every curl; it took a long time to make the Shirley Temple-look ringlets. Until this day I still love having someone fix my hair—just ask my daughters! My mother was also very supportive of my musical involvements and always took me to all my events.

Mom also modeled for me how to entertain guests. She was very English and everything had to be just right; before guests came, we had to dust and polish immaculately. This helped prepare me for entertaining in my adult years. She was basically a meat, potatoes and gravy cook for daily meals; the first time I tasted casseroles was when I went to college, and because I hadn't grown up on them, I loved them!

Mom was a very beautiful lady; she easily could have won a beauty contest. One day when I was about 12 (but looking more like 16), she and I dressed up and walked to the bus stop so we could go to downtown Detroit to shop and probably see a movie. A handsome young man driving a convertible pulled up in front of us and started flirting with Mom. I got disgusted with him and told him to "get lost." His response to Mom was, "Tell your older sister to leave us alone." Then the bus came.

One summer when I was 14, Dad bought a camping trailer and a canoe. He hooked them up to our car. Then, with all our gear, including Mom, Bud (10), Jerry (2), and 4-month-old Nate, we squeezed in. We drove to a campground in the bay of Lake Superior in Upper Michigan. It was here that Dad taught me how to canoe, but warned me not to take the canoe out alone. But one afternoon I just couldn't resist, and soon I was canoeing in the bay, not realizing that a storm was brewing. The wind was carrying me out further and further. Then I heard Dad calling from the shore and motioning to me to cross the bay. He drove the car around the bay and picked me up on the other side. Again God was protecting me, even in my disobedience and foolishness.

On this same trip, we were driving on some of the back roads in the mountain area when we spotted a bear approaching us. Dad stopped the car and got out with his movie camera. Mom enticed the bear to come to the car window and while Dad filmed the event, Mom fed the bear crackers out of a small opening in the window. Bud and I squealed with excitement! This was the greatest family vacation I can ever remember.

Although my father was a Design Engineer for Vickers, Inc., he loved to spend his evenings studying the Bible. In our basement he set up a large drawing board where he developed his Bible charts. His chart on the Tabernacle in the wilderness, along with a study guide, has been translated into four languages and used by teachers in Bible Colleges. He wrote some other booklets as well, but I think his autobiography, "God's Fugitive," by Glenn M. Jones, is the best.

I loved to watch him work on his charts. When I was about 12, he paid me a quarter for each chart I colored for him. When he would give lectures in churches, he would put up a very large chart of his subject matter and also give each attendee a small copy of the chart. I believe some of his booklets are still in print by Kregel Publications in Grand Rapids, Michigan.

Dad also loved to play the guitar. I'm told that he balanced his chair on one leg while simultaneously playing the guitar and the harmonica. I remember when he got an electric guitar and would entertain the family with his Hawaiian songs as well as hymns in the church.

One of my fondest memories when visiting my grandparent's house was watching all my uncles and aunts along with my father get out their banjos, guitars, and mandolins for a "jam session," as they call it today. They would sing and play for hours. Perhaps that was the beginning of my love for music. In fact, I recently learned that Dad gave guitar lessons to my mother. Perhaps that was the beginning of their romance.

After a brief courtship, Dad, who was 23 years old, asked my 16-year-old mother's father for her hand in marriage. My grandfather refused, but I am told that they became pregnant so her father would have to let them get married. When I was 12, I asked my mother when their anniversary was and she told me August, but then I asked Dad and he said September. I was born May 1st. Being a good mathematician, I figured out that there was a problem—that's when I went to the "wisest" person I knew—my favorite cousin, who was almost three years older than me, for the answers. She then told me how my parents got married because they were expecting me. This was quite a shock to me. In my young mind I surmised that I was the problem for all their unhappiness evident by their constant arguing. I felt so guilty! I just tried to put it out of my mind and pour myself even more into my music.

********* Music

I need to regress back to when I was seven when a different side of my life began. My great aunt gave us an upright player piano. I was soon taking piano lessons and learning how to pour out my love and emotions through my playing. To say I loved playing the piano would be an understatement. It was my life. Only once did my Mother ever have to remind me to practice. All she had to say was, "Ruthie, if you are not going to practice then you are not going to take lessons." That was enough to get me to focus again on practicing.

I apparently was progressing rapidly on the piano, as I became the accompanist for our school choir when I was in fourth grade. We had a very strict music teacher, Miss Modelle. She really made us kids learn music and developed us into a great choir. By eighth grade we were so good that we got to sing on a radio program as our reward. In eighth grade, I also auditioned to accompany the elementary school district orchestra and got the job. This meant traveling by bus to other schools and performing with the orchestra in many concerts in the Detroit area.

Because I was in a piano recital every year, my parents patiently sat through hours and hours of performances. When I was 12, four of us played a two-piano duo with eight hands at the Detroit Music Hall; this was a great honor.

I loved to perform and looked for opportunities to do this. In eighth grade, I thought it would be fun to "act out" a popular song, "Shine on Harvest Moon." I got two other girls involved—one dancing, the other singing—in our own little Vaudeville show number! I had never seen anything like this, so I thought I was inventing a new musical form! Soon after that I auditioned to play in a talent show on the radio (no TV in those days). I remember playing, "Malaguena."

In high school I played for the choir and a small group called the "Falconaires". We played and sang for clubs and variety shows all over Detroit.

Another part of my piano performances was to play before a judge at Michigan State each year. I finally achieved the highest grade— which entitled me to perform at the State level. That very same day, I performed in the evening at my high school talent show and WON! This entitled me to be part of a team—one performer from each of the six schools in our league. The rest of the year I just had to turn in my homework for some of my classes, and then I was free to go practice for that hour. What a joy for me to have that much time to practice!

********** Eighth Grade
A lot of changes took place in eighth grade, as our beloved but very strict principal retired and we got a young man just out of college. Our eighth grade class started testing the new principal, doing things in class like throwing books across the room. When we would end up in his office for our "punishment," he would just talk to us and tell us not to do it again.

That method just didn't work because we were used to strictness, so we lost respect for him and did just as we pleased. I began wearing lipstick and hair ribbons to school, which the former principal outlawed. One day I forgot to wash off the lipstick and Dad saw me. Again he angrily told me to wash it off and not wear it again! Some of my friends began trying smoking, but I never did—seriously, I never

21

tried smoking until I was 16, and I hated it so much that I never did it again.

My classmate, Nancy, lived across the street from me and one day on the way to school she slipped me a package. It was a bra! I was already about a 34b breast but didn't know I should be wearing a bra. I guess she saw my need and wanted to help me out.

Nancy invited me to her birthday party to be held in her basement one Saturday night. My parents were very trusting and let me go. Wow! If they only knew what went on at that party they would have been shocked. Kids I had never seen before showed up. I was soon caught up in the excitement and started dancing with one of the guys. But, a classmate of mine, Marvin, kept his eye on me. He was already 16 and more "worldly wise" than I was. He saw the guy I was dancing with ask me to go for a walk with him. I was about to say "yes" when I saw Marvin shake his head "no." Fortunately I had the sense not to go. Marvin was my Guardian Angel that night. I can only imagine what might have happened. The guy I was dancing with saw Marvin shake his head "no" and picked a fight with him.

For our eighth grade graduation trip we went by train to Washington D.C. My mother made me a special three-piece eveningwear pajama set in a shiny blue satin. Wow! I just had to show it off, so on the train I changed into it and paraded around enjoying the attention of everyone.

Altogether we were about 25 kids and 8 chaperones. I know the chaperones were watching me carefully. (Don't you wonder why?) When we got to the hotel there was a high school group also staying at this hotel and they were having a dance that night. In the lobby that afternoon one of the guys in the group began flirting with me and invited me to come to the dance that evening. I really looked older than 14. Unbeknown to me one of the chaperones was watching. I had no plans to go to the dance, but the rumor somehow got around that I went. How funny it was a few hours later when the chaperone knocked at my door and was shocked to see that I had just taken a shower and had my hair up in a towel. She began berating me for going to the dance—I'm sure she just didn't know what else to say as I obviously wasn't there!

********** **Moving to Farmington**

Soon our little bungalow was too small for our expanding family. Jerry was born when I was 11 and Nate was born 18 months later. Jerry would grow up to follow his dad in the engineering field. When Nate was seven, I suggested he take piano lessons. Today he is a professional soft jazz musician. Bud married a girl whose father was a vice president of the Ford Motor Company. Bud eventually became the Inventory Analyst of the company.

By the next fall we had moved to Farmington, MI. My parents had a three-bedroom house built into a hill so there was a walkout basement leading to a cement veranda. The backyard extended about 500 feet to a little creek. Dad set up his archery equipment there and would spend hours practicing for the biggest event of the year: deer hunting. As far as I can remember, he got his buck every year. Sometimes the men would even take their wives with them. During those times Bud and I got to go to our grandparents' house to stay. But I remember Mom growing tired of having to cook venison. Sometimes the meat was tough and dry.

Moving to this new house out of the big city was a whole new world for me. My pre-school tendencies of shyness now enveloped me again. I found it hard to make new friends. One day in English class a girl sitting a few rows back from me passed me a love note. The teacher saw it and had me bring the note to her. When she read it and saw who sent it, she told me to stay after class. She explained to me that this note was inappropriate and cautioned me to be careful about a friendship with her. I was very naive, but I was careful after that. But Irene kept sending me notes and inviting me to her house. She was two years older than me; her hands shook most of the time and she just seemed rather odd so I didn't pay much attention to her.

One day our class was playing basketball in the gym, which was also the auditorium; the huge curtains on the stage were closed. Someone threw a basketball to me that landed on the stage and rolled behind the curtain. I ran up the stairs behind the curtain on the right side of the stage and Irene ran up the other stairs on the other side of the stage. We both got to the center trying to grab the ball when suddenly she hugged me and kissed me. As if that wasn't bad enough, someone at that moment pulled the curtain open for all the class to see! I was SO humiliated. I didn't know what to do. No one came to help me and I never told anyone about it. This certainly didn't help me make friends! Irene soon left school; I never knew the reason. But I am so thankful for my English teacher. To me this was evident that God's angel was protecting me again in my naivety.

********** **High School**
One night soon after I got my driver's license I asked Dad if I could drive over to my friend's house to study for a test. But I lied; actually I went to the school dance. Although Dad let me go, I'm sure he was suspicious. Later at the dance Dad showed up. I was having a great time on the dance floor until someone whispered to me, "Ruth, your Dad is here!" I was really scared. But he just told me to go home immediately. Dancing was considered a sin in my church at that time. I don't remember him ever bringing it up again. He was a man of few words, but he probably increased his prayers for me!

After my junior year, I went to Bible Camp again and came home with a new desire to really follow Jesus. I quit hanging around with the crowd at school who were now into smoking and drinking. I had tried to share my faith with my best friend, but she just mocked me; that was the end of our friendship. I remember feeling so alone at school. There was no one I could really hang out with. I felt so sad that my friends had deserted me. Jeannie lived 10 miles away now and went to a different high school.

But it didn't take me long to see what God had for me to do. I decided to start a Bible Club. We were not allowed to meet in the school building, so I got permission from the church across the street to use their facilities. I found a group of new friends who, like me, were excited to follow Jesus and be a witness for Him in our school.

It was at this time that God gave me a really special gift—a baby sister, Karen Ann. After having three brothers, this was a great joy! Three years later, Lois Kristine would be born. Both of these girls are very gifted in the arts and have found their careers in this field.

********** **Boys**

I also tried my luck at theater and played the part of a snobbish rich girl in the play, "Here Comes Charlie". After that everybody thought I really was a snob. I was a rather quiet person in school, which was mistaken, I think, for being snobbish. The boys in my class decided to nominate me for Homecoming Queen. What an honor! What I didn't know was that this was a mean trick. They all agreed not to vote for me. Of course I voted for myself—wouldn't you? When the votes were tallied and I only got one vote, they roared in laughter, and I ran out of the room crying. I was convinced that boys could be so mean! Somehow I survived the humiliation. This now confirmed their belief that I was a snob!

The boys always seem to be teasing me; when I wore a sweater to school, they would say, "Hubba, Hubba!" (a common phrase for: "What a hot chick!") But I never dated any of them; I just brushed them off and quit wearing sweaters to school.

I did date, but not boys from my class. There were three boys in my church around my age and I dated all of them at least once, but the one I liked a lot was Bob Erickson. He had a cool car—a Model A Ford with a rumble seat. He was three years older than I was and was ready to settle down. On my eighteenth birthday he asked me to marry him and gave me a diamond. Soon after that, he left for the army and I left for college.

********** **Graduation**

When graduation came, I was given the "Music Student of the Year" award. Perhaps this helped me decide on music instead of a theatrical career.

It was soon time for me to choose a college. I was bent on going to the prestigious Julliard School of Music in New York. My father was very concerned about this, but instead of approaching me with a negative **attitude**, he was very wise. He suggested I go to a Christian college for one year and then I could go on to Julliard if I wanted to. I was disappointed, but I loved my father and respected his wisdom greatly. I decided to follow his advice. This decision would alter the course of my life in ways I could never have fathomed.

Chapter 3

FRED'S STORY
(1933-1958)

TRAIN HITS CAR OF FOUR, ONE FATALITY

My early life was filled with tragedies. My father, Frederick George Thomas, Sr., of Lebanese decent, was killed in a train accident at age 22 when I was just three months old. The above were the headlines in the morning newspaper in Norfolk, VA, March, 1934. This news would change my life forever. My mother, Modina, only 17 years old, struggled greatly to work and take care of me. Often I was cared for by my dear aunt living nearby in Norfolk, VA, or by my Lebanese family who lived a few houses away.

Another tragedy I had was falling out of my baby carriage and cracking my head open when I was about 18 months old. I still have the scars. Then another near tragedy was when I ran out into traffic at the age of two and a truck ran over me; however, I was unharmed because I fell under the truck between the wheels. When I was seven, I started to dart out between parked cars to get into my uncle's car parked across the busy street. Fortunately, someone grabbed me from behind, saving me from the fast moving traffic that certainly would have been my demise. My guardian angel was really watching over me.

God certainly had a plan for my life that nothing could stop.

Soon Modina fell in love with Buren F. Sprague, and they were married when I was only two years old. A year later, Charles Theodore was born into this new union and we moved to a farm near Sheldon, Wisconsin. This was quite a change of pace for a confined little city boy to have the freedom to roam around a sprawling farm. Four years later the last living boy of this family was born – Buren Jr, who was known as "Toots" during his childhood. My brothers and I had multiple great times together feeding the animals, milking the cows, and even helping with the harvests.

We lived on three different farms until I was ten years old when we moved to Racine, Wisconsin. When I was six, my mother's sister, Aunt Ernestine in Norfolk, begged to let me come and live with her for a year (she had no children). This is where I learned to be a proper Southern boy, to go to church every Sunday, and to be confirmed in the Catholic Church. It was after mass one Sunday, as mentioned above, that I ran out between two cars into traffic and was "saved" by a man who grabbed me from behind just in time.

During some of those early years we were "farmed out" to families while our folks worked in Chicago off and on. One family whom we lived with were Chippewa Indians; when they would drive the three miles into town on a horse drawn buckboard and we were left alone, we helped ourselves to the government rationed coffee and sugar.

During the Second World War, the government mandated that only one family member could run the farm — the other would have to serve in the military or work in a factory. Because Buren and his brother Don co-owned the farm, it was decided that Buren would take his family to Racine, Wisconsin where he found a job working in a defense plant foundry, Bell City. Modina also went to work for J. I. Case manufacturing military tanks. Later on she had other jobs including cooking in a restaurant (she was a fabulous cook).

It was the last two years on the farm, however, that were much more significant to my early spiritual life. My grandparents (Buren's parents) always stopped by the farm to take my brothers, Ted and Toots, and me to their Pentecostal Sunday school and church with them. Just before I joined my parents in Racine, I attended a Vacation Bible School and sensed my need to know Jesus. My parents did not nurture this childlike trust, so I began to run with the ruffians in my neighborhood, getting involved in all kinds of mischievous deeds.

However, one of the neighborhood kids, who became my best friend, Al Christensen, did attend a local Baptist Church and invited me to go along with him to Sunday school. My attending was sporadic, but I was hearing more and more about what it meant to be a follower of Jesus. Al and I were real buddies and we did everything together. We spent a lot of time playing in his basement during the winter months, and running around the neighborhood with other boys our age.

We also got into petty thievery and stashing our stuff in our hideout. One day at school when I was 14, I got called to the office and was confronted with the reality of the wrong I was doing. There were policemen in plain clothes waiting for me. They asked, "What is this Frederick street gang we are hearing about?" I thought they were asking me to join a "club". We never referred to ourselves as the "Frederick Street Gang". But we lived on the corner of Prospect and Frederick Street, so they thought I was smart mouthing when I asked them if they were starting a neighborhood boys club. I soon found out they were private detectives and they had raided our "fort" and found some of the items we had stolen. They warned me if I continued to do this it would mean Juvenile Court. I always thought it was my youngest brother, Toots, who squealed on us, but just a couple of years ago when I asked him about it, he said it was another kid in the neighborhood who was upset because we wouldn't allow him in our "gang."

I was really worried about what my Mom would do when she heard about this from the police. When I needed discipline, she would take the rubber hose off our washing machine lid and whip me with it. So, I decided I better tell her what I had done when I got home and take the beating. However, when I told my Mom with many sobs and tears, she realized I was very repentant and didn't whip me. She warned me, "Just don't do that again."

This experience caused me to turn to the Lord more than I had ever done before. People in the church, like Ken Parsons Sr. and Art Kastensen, really nurtured me and treated me like a son. Art even paid my way to Bible camp that summer when I was 14. At that camp I did some heart-searching about my life. While listening to a missionary from the Belgian Congo speak, I felt she was speaking right to me. I sensed the Holy Spirit say to me, "I am inviting you to give your life to serve me in a foreign land, and to help people who have never heard of Me experience the Abundant Life that I will give them."

Along with about 12 other guys and gals, I went forward that night and gave my life to do this very thing. From that day on I set my mind and heart on that goal. I never looked back! From then on I focused on preparing myself to be a missionary.

Now a reformed, or rather transformed, teenager, I decided to go back to the YMCA where I had been kicked out at age 12 and to apply for a job as a junior secretary. The director, Raymond Vance, had heard of the change in my life and my desire to become a missionary, and hired me to work under the supervision of the secretary, Fred Fuhrman. I worked there every day after school during my three years at Horlick High School and learned much about management, dealing with people, and sharing my faith. Mr. Fuhrman helped me decide where to go to college as he explained the difference between a college and university, and of course wanted me to go to William and Mary, his alma mater. Mr. Vance wanted me to go to Roger Williams University and train to be a YMCA director "where I could be a missionary in Egypt as a director." But I felt the Lord wanted me to be doing direct evangelism, which would include establishing churches that would be self-governing, self-supporting, and self-propagating.

During the summer months, I worked back on the farm for my uncle and grandfather in Sheldon. I was able to save a little money for college in this way.

All this time Al and I continued to be best friends; one night we went together with the other youth from our church to visit another church in Kenosha, a city south of Racine. There we heard about two Christian colleges: Wheaton College and Bethel College. Al and I decided to apply to Wheaton first, but we couldn't get in until the spring quarter and Al, being a year older than me, could have possibly been drafted into the Korean War. So we decided to apply to Bethel College and we were accepted for the fall quarter.

In the fall of 1951, Al and I, with great excitement, headed to Bethel College in St. Paul, Minnesota. Al's parents drove us there to begin our training for what God had planned for the future. The best was yet to come! Al also had a sense of calling to serve God full-time in some capacity. After graduation, Al spent 13 years working for Young Life Organization, which establishes Christian Clubs in high schools all over the country. Then he continued his studies and eventually became a successful Christian family therapist.

At Bethel College, I was talked into going out for football and made the team. After sitting on the bench for almost the entire first game, I finally got a chance to play for 60 seconds. I threw a 30-yard pass that was incomplete; the game ended with a penalty for "roughing the passer," and they gave us one more play. I threw the same pass play for 30 yards and the receiver ran another 30 yards for a touchdown. We still lost 13 to 6 but it was a great victory for me. After that, I was a starter for the rest of my four years of college football.

I wasn't the best student the first couple of years in college. I had a hard time settling down to really study — besides being known for sports, including basketball and track, I was known as a prankster as well. I won't go into any of my shenanigans at this time, except I was accused of almost burning down the seminary building on Bethel's campus, and was banned from the building for the rest of my freshman year.

During fall football practice, I met my future wife, Ruth, who was on campus for freshman orientation week. I still didn't totally settle down until we married the next summer, and I started getting serious about my studies and was able to graduate from college with a B average. Married life was good for me in numerous ways.

I was a self-supporting student and found time to drive a public school bus for six years, from my sophomore year in college through my three years as a theological student at Bethel Seminary. Ruth also worked after we were married, as she also pursued her studies and graduated with an elementary education degree from the University of Minnesota at the same time I graduated from Bethel Seminary in 1958.

I was ordained as a Baptist minister the summer of 1958. That September, the Baptist General Conference (now known as

"Converge") commissioned us under the auspices of Faith Baptist Church, Royal Oak, MI, as missionary appointees to the Philippines, where we started our mission career in December 1958.

Chapter 4
(1952-1953)

COLLEGE
"Each for the other; both for the Lord"

In the fall of 1952, before there were freeways, my parents drove me the 700 miles to Bethel College in St. Paul, Minnesota. It was a great place for me to be; I liked being 700 miles from home. Only once in my lifetime had I ever been outside the state of Michigan, so this was like going to the North Pole. I loved the independence! I could finally spread my wings!

Immediately I got involved in music. In fact, I played a piano solo at the Freshman Orientation where Fred saw me for the first time. He was on campus a week early for football practice. He and his buddies decided to sneak into the freshman mixer and check out the chicks. I guess I was the one he picked.

That year, besides taking all the required classes, I also studied piano and organ. But I soon dropped out of organ — I just found it too confining and mechanical. I was used to moving all over the keyboard, not having to deal with two keyboards plus a set of pedals.

I also auditioned for the Women's Chorus and enjoyed singing the kind of music I never knew existed -- Cantatas, Oratorios, and Sacred Classics, as well as a genre of current Christian music. In the spring, we went on a three-weekend concert tour of churches in the Midwest. What fun!

I was very impressed with the kind of Christianity I found at this school -- so positive, so real, as though God was really present in you and around you, and would really speak to you if you were listening! I began to long for more of this kind of Christianity in my life. One night during this Orientation week, I rededicated my life to Jesus.

After that I felt so free and happy, and my heart and mind were ready to receive whatever He had for me.

Six weeks later was Missions Week at the school. During each morning Chapel service and each evening service, we had missionaries from all over the world share how God was changing lives in their sphere of ministry. My heart was deeply touched each night and I began to sense that God was calling me to be a missionary.

Following each evening service I would go to the practice rooms and play the piano, then cry out to God, "Lord, are you asking me to give up my music to be a missionary? Music is my first love; how can I do that?" Finally on the last night, I surrendered my music to the Lord. I was reminded that one cannot serve two masters. Either God must be Lord of all, or He is not Lord AT all! I couldn't see the future, but, now that God was Lord of my life, I finally had peace in my heart.

Fred and I had one of those storybook romances; Fred was a football player and I was a cheerleader. What I first remember about him were his flirtations. He would call me "Cutie" and other such sweet words. He was also very funny; quite a "cut-up" as they use to say.

At Bethel College there was a Swedish celebration each year in the fall. It was like "Sadie Hawkins's Day"-- girls got to ask the boys out on a date. The school planned a variety show program for this occasion, but girls usually did more than that; they took the guy out for dinner, made him a corsage, and often took him to a Lakers basketball game.

But being only eighteen and lonely, I was enjoying being pursued by this tall, dark and handsome football player. My problem was that I was still engaged to Bob. Then I got an idea! There was a boy in my class who also engaged to a girl back home so I thought maybe it would be okay for us to go together to all the activities just as friends. So I wrote to my fiancée and asked his permission. He reluctantly gave in. As I looked at how much money I was going to have to spend, I decided it wasn't worth it to spend all that money on someone I didn't even think I would enjoy being with. So why not just ask this goofy guy, Fred, to go with me? At least I knew I would have a fun evening!

That should make it "okay" right? So that's exactly what I did. We went with my roommate and her boyfriend to a Lakers basketball game. We had so much fun! I knew I was beginning to like him after that night. We started studying together and talking a lot about ourselves. I found out that Fred had felt God's call to be a missionary when he was 14. I soon realized I had a very big problem!

While I was home for Christmas I received a dozen yellow roses from this Romeo. My mother was elated! She did not want me to marry this other guy, as she didn't like his family. So I had to tell her all about Fred. I got to see Bob while I was home for Christmas, and I realized I really didn't love him. We had grown apart during the months we were separated. I was too young and immature for this commitment. I broke the engagement when I got back to college and began seeing my true love!

For Valentines that year Fred wrote me the following poem:

First Date!

"My heart is yearning and really burning
For the love you have for me.
I only ask, this one small task
That you my Valentine will be!"

This was just written on a piece of paper, but worth a million dollars to me!

On spring break, Fred drove the 700 miles to my home in Farmington, Michigan to ask my father for my hand in marriage.

That was a funny scenario: My dad and Fred were talking in the living room; they had so much in common since Fred was studying to be a missionary. My mother and I were in the kitchen listening. I was getting perturbed, as Fred wasn't getting around to the point, so I told my mother what he was trying to ask. My mother called my dad to the bedroom and told him what Fred desired to ask him, so when my dad came back to the living room, he invited Fred to go with him to the backyard to learn how to shoot archery. It was in that context that Fred finally asked for my hand in marriage.

On May 1st, Fred asked me to marry him and put a beautiful diamond on my finger. His mother had given him the ring from her first husband who was killed in a train wreck and was Fred's biological father. Fred had the diamonds re-set for a ring for me.

Fred was quite a "Casanova". During our many weeks separation during the summer he wrote me over 20 letters (I still have them). Here is a sample of one:

"Darling; All I want to repeat and repeat is that I LOVE YOU. Take me in your arms and hold me and squeeze me until I can't breathe a breath...." Wow! What a lover!

We were separated for the summer while I went home to prepare for our August wedding, and Fred went to his home in Racine, Wisconsin to work as a grounds keeper in a cemetery. I got my old job back -- wrapping fresh meat in the supermarkets. But Fred's job did not last all summer because of the dry weather, so he came to Michigan and found work in construction.

On August 29, 1953 at 5 pm we were married at the First Baptist Church of Farmington, Michigan. Cousin Mary Beth was my matron of honor; Pat Larson, my college roommate, and Jean Allaire, my life-long friend, were my bridesmaids. My darling little 2½-year-old sister, Karen, was my flower girl. Fred's best friend, Al Christensen was our best man; Ron Christensen and Norman Moore were the groomsmen. Fred's brother, Chuck (Ted), and my brother, Bud, were ushers.

It was a lovely wedding. We had only one glitch: little Karen began crying when we wanted her to walk ahead of me down the aisle. But she finally agreed to follow me down the aisle scattering the flower pedals. We should have known then that she would be an artist — always doing things "out-of-the-box."

We bought a black, 1949 Studebaker Business Coupe with the money we had saved. This was perfect for our needs. The area behind the front seat was completely open all the way through to the trunk. We packed our wedding gifts in there, and headed to St. Paul, Minnesota to continue our schooling. We only had $100 for our honeymoon, but what was important was that we were together. We found a stately old home where they rented out rooms right near the Lake Michigan Sand Dunes for $3.00 a night. We enjoyed three days of bliss, sliding down the sand dunes and just having fun together. In just a few days we would arrive in St. Paul. The "two shall be one flesh"; God had truly brought us together with a common purpose and passion in life. We were ready to share our lives and work hard to achieve our common goal -- to *"go into all the world"* and proclaim the Good News about God's love to whatever place God would send us.

Chapter 5
(1953-1958)

PREPARATION
"Lord, grant that I may always desire more than I can accomplish."
-- Michelangelo

When we arrived at Bethel College, we quickly found a third-floor apartment in the attic of a nearby house. I'll never forget the day I baked a pie, then left to do some quick shopping. When I returned home, I discovered I had forgotten my key. By the time I found the owners and borrowed another key, my pie was a pile of ashes! So began my life as a new bride!

After living there for a month, we moved to a basement apartment right across the street from the college. It was sufficient for us, and there was a small private room, so we invited my mother to come for a visit; she had never been to a football game before so it was fun taking her to Bethel's Homecoming game. Of course, Fred was playing in it, so that made it extra special. I remember her asking questions like, "Why do the players get in a huddle?" I believe she enjoyed seeing her oldest daughter happily married. But instead of me giving her a grandchild, she is the one who delivered a darling little girl a year later: beautiful little Lois Christine was born August 7, 1954.

From 1953 to 1958, we enjoyed many different pursuits. We both worked besides going to school. Fred worked part-time driving school bus for seven years, and I worked full time at the Grain Terminal Co-op for one year. Then I went back to school for one year to finish my 2-year degree in Religious Education at Bethel. I also taught piano during that year and continued teaching for the next five years. My next employment was working for the International Harvester Corporation.

In 1955, Fred graduated from Bethel College with a major in Sociology and minors in Philosophy and Psychology. I graduated from Bethel College in a 2-year program with an ARE (Associate in Religious Education).

We lived on a very tight budget; to save money we would pick up bushels of green beans, tomatoes, and corn to can in the fall, which was usually enough to last us through the school year. We could buy 3 pounds of hamburger for a dollar, so I put my creativity to work using hamburger in a variety of ways. We stayed healthy and happy.

After our first year of married life, we were able to move again, this time to the married couples' dorm on campus. Our apartment had a miniscule kitchen, a small bathroom, and a living area where the Murphy bed had to be pulled down from the wall each night. The apartment was small, but just right for two people. There were three floors of married couples, so we had a lot of fun together. Our best friends lived across the hall -- Dale and Carolyn Nystrom. Dale was in seminary with Fred, and Carolyn was a nurse. Dale was-also a great vocalist. I was his accompanist when he was asked to sing at various churches. How excited we were when they had a little girl, Jodie. We enjoyed being Aunt and Uncle to her for the next four years. (Presently, they live near San Francisco.) — We were able to pay all our own school expenses and even buy a new yellow hardtop convertible Studebaker the second year I was working.

I began thinking seriously about what kind of additional training I needed in order to be a missionary. I hadn't bothered to ask God about it; I just presumed that the best way to help people was to become a nurse. But as I was filling out the application, my heart was heavy. I had no propensity toward nursing. God spoke to my heart and reminded me of what my gifting was. I loved music, but I also loved working with children. At this time I was helping with church programs for kids. I even worked in downtown St. Paul with underprivileged kids for one year. So, I tore up the application and the next day went to the University of Minnesota and applied for entrance in their teaching program.

In addition to working very hard to complete my teaching degree over the next 2 years (plus one summer), I also auditioned to study piano. After playing in front of about 10 piano professors, Dr. Weisner, a former student of Rachmaninoff, chose me to study with him. Rachmaninoff happened to be one of my favorite composers, so I was really privileged to study under Dr. Weisner. He taught me so much about technique and being attentive to detail. He was one of those fortunate enough to have escaped Hitler's rage against Jews.

During that summer I invited two of my brothers, Jerry who was 10, and Nate who was 8 to come for a visit. Fred was working the night shift loading delivery trucks; I was in summer school all morning every day so I took the boys with me to class! Since we lived in a tiny studio apartment, the boys slept on the bed during the night while Fred was at work, and I slept on the sofa. We had a great time together. I also remember making them cowboy shirts for Christmas. At this writing, Jerry is retired from a design engineering career, and Nate teaches Jazz and has many weekend gigs playing at weddings, dances, etc. They are now both grandpas, and it's fun seeing them in this role.

In my last year of school, I got to do my practicum in the fourth grade of an elementary school near the University campus. I particularly enjoyed working with the students struggling with learning, but my teacher encouraged me to challenge the top students to excel instead. The second semester I did my practice teaching in a sixth grade class. Although the teacher and I didn't hit it off very well, I learned how important it is to motivate students and to encourage them gently with suggestions on how to improve, and not just to chastise them for their errors.

Two piano duo with Bob Carlson playing "Concerto #2" by Saint Saens In 1956

One of the fun things I did was travel with the Bethel Male Chorus by bus on three-week tours for two spring concert series. I was the piano soloist and accompanist (just me and 38 men on a bus for three weeks), and Fred was the business manager. What an experience! We gave concerts in churches throughout the Midwest in 1957. In 1958, we gave concerts along the way to California and back. While in California, we met Dr. and Mrs. Keith Knopf, who invited us to their home for dinner. We told them of our call to missions, and from then on they became a vital part of our lives for the next fifty or more years.

These years of adjusting to marriage were not always easy. Both of us were very busy in our separate lives of school and work, but we tried to enjoy special times on Sunday at Como Park, which was within walking distance of Bethel College. We also took two canoe trips up to the Boundary waters with another couple.

One time we canoed to our camping grounds on one of the islands. It was still early afternoon so we decided to do some fishing before setting up camp. We found a Walleye hole and began pulling in the Walleyes as fast as we could. We put them on a fish line and dangled them over the side. I believe this is the best-tasting fish in the world. Our mouths were watering as we headed back to our campgrounds to cook them. Suddenly we realized we were lost; it was dusk now and hard to see which of the many islands was ours. After wandering for some time, we saw a campfire and called to the people asking directions.

They told us they had seen us unloading our camping gear earlier just across from them! Tired and hungry we finally pulled our canoes onto land. Then we looked for our fish. To our dismay, the fish line holding them must have broken or twisted off; we never got to eat our catch! The next day it rained all day so we stayed in our tent and played our favorite card game, Rook. Laughter and play are the best medicine for heavy hearts and rainy days!

 When Fred was in his second year (middle year) at Bethel Seminary, he was asked to be the weekend pastor of the oldest Swedish Baptist Church in Minnesota, Scandia Baptist, located in Waconia. So, each Saturday for the next year and a half, we would drive to Waconia to spend the night with members of the church, and Fred would preach each Sunday.

Every Sunday, someone from the church would have to get there early to heat the little church building by starting a fire in the wood stove. We enjoyed being with this small congregation of about 40 people each week; they were so good to us and we learned much

41

about what it means to be pastors. A few years later, this congregation had mostly died out, and the remaining descendents donated the building to the new Bethel Campus. Now every time we visit Bethel, we see the little chapel and it brings back beautiful memories of our short time there.

June of 1958 was the time we both graduated. I graduated from the University of Minnesota with a Bachelor of Science in Elementary Education. Fred graduated from Bethel Theological Seminary with a Bachelor of Divinity. We now felt well prepared to spread our wings, using our training and God-given gifts to seek to make a difference for good in this needy world. How surprised we were to find out our preparation had just begun; it was the start of a life-long education.

Chapter 6
(1958)

TO ISLANDS BEYOND
"The islands are calling to you with hope..."

One of the aspects of preparing to go to the Philippines was visiting churches and telling them of our passion to serve God as missionaries. I'll never forget one particular week when we were helping with a rural church's VBS. We were invited to visit various homes for our meals, as well as some of the farms to have an afternoon snack. On one of those afternoons, we arrived at a nearby farm to find they had prepared an afternoon "snack" of sandwiches and salads – enough for a full meal. The men had come in from the fields to join us. It was a great time of getting to know these lovely and gracious people, who encouraged us to "eat our fill."

Unfortunately, we were scheduled to have dinner at a widow's home at 6:00 pm, and were shocked to learn that she had spent a great sum of money to honor us with a steak dinner. We tried our best to be hospitable and eat her delicious food, but were already so full from the "snacks" at the farmhouse that it was quite difficult. In fact, Fred was so full that he had to excuse himself to avoid embarrassing our host; he then went to the bathroom and "lost" his second meal.

But let me back up a bit: how did we decide to go to the Philippines? When Fred received his call to be a missionary, the missionary lady who spoke was from the Congo, so he thought he was also called to go to the Congo. His first thought was to see if his home church, a German Baptist Church, had any mission work in the Congo. The only kind of mission work they had in Africa was in the Cameroons teaching in a school. Fred just didn't feel that was his calling.

Next, his missions professor in Seminary, Walfred Danielson, asked Fred if he would consider going out under the Baptist General Conference (the denomination of Bethel College & Seminary). Desiring to be open to God's leading, we filled out applications with the BGC. Soon after this we read an article in the "Standard," their monthly publication.

Roy Nelson, a missionary in the Philippines whom Fred knew, wrote the article, which told about the need for missionaries in that country. Fred's heart was touched with this need and I concurred when I read the article. Later we were asked to come to the BGC headquarters in Chicago for an interview with the Mission Board Committee, and, after a lengthy interview, we were asked, "Would you be willing to go to the Philippines, if we appointed you there?" God had already prepared our hearts in this direction. We said "yes." This was in April of 1958.

Soon after that, Fred was ordained by the Royal Oak Baptist Church, in Berkeley, Michigan. Later that month, Fred and I were appointed by the BGC Foreign Mission Board as missionaries to the Philippines at their Annual Conference. We were scheduled to leave in December with returning missionaries Andy and Elvie Nelson, and new missionaries, classmates Dick and Elenor Varberg and their baby, Paul.

We spent the next four months speaking at various churches and telling about our call to the Philippines. A number of churches decided to make us their "personal missionary" family. They helped us gather many of the supplies we needed and pack them in barrels for shipping. The First Baptist Church in Lakewood, CA was one of those churches. We had become friends with Dr. and Mrs. Keith Knopf a few months earlier on our Male Chorus Tour and they were very instrumental in our being selected. Actually, Pastor Harold Carlson wanted us to be members of this church, but we had already committed our membership to Faith Baptist in Royal Oak, Michigan.

It was a grand day when we three couples sailed on the President Cleveland passenger liner. A great number of friends from many churches were at the pier, cheering us on and praying for us. We were saying goodbye to friends and family for four years.

Our first ocean vessel experience was in very rough water -- in fact we were told December was the worst month of the year for ocean travel! Fred and Dick learned about this the hard way. They couldn't even finish a meal before they had to run up on deck and lose it all.

But we did have a lot of fun on the 21-day voyage. We enjoyed a stopover for three days in Hawaii and rented a van for touring all over the island. I remember seeing trees with vines hanging down and wondering if Tarzan lived there. Oh, happy day when we got to the Philippines! We arrived in Manila on December 28, 1958.

We were reminded of these words from Scripture: "The plans I have for you," says the Lord, "are for good and not for evil, to give you a future and a hope" (Jeremiah 29:11). Little did we know at that time what an exciting life lie ahead of us!

Chapter 7
(1959-1962)

A NEW LAND -- A NEW CULTURE
"Remember in the dark what God taught you in the light"

As our ship pulled into Manila Bay on December 28, 1958, we were filled with excitement and anticipation of all God had in store for us in the years to come. I remember staying at the OMF (Overseas Missionary Fellowship) guest house; we slept on straw mattresses with no mosquito nets. The next morning I counted 63 mosquito bites on my legs! I could see we were going to have to make many adjustments to our new environment.

Fred and I had both established a pattern in our marriage of working very hard; it seemed like we were always on the go. This pattern didn't stop after we reached the Philippines. We spent 8 hours a day just studying the language. We were determined to learn to speak fluently in the Cebuano dialect.

Each morning, we had a private tutor for two hours to teach us grammar. Each afternoon was spent working with an informant on actual speaking -- intonations and accent. We tried to use as much of the language as we knew, practicing on people in the neighborhood . and in the church. I would also play volleyball in the yard with the children in the neighborhood; this helped me learn to understand how they spoke.

One evening I saw a new man at the church. Our tutor had told us that her son was coming to visit so I thought I would ask this young man if he was her son. I introduced myself and then asked, "*Ikaw ba ang lalaki ni Mrs. Lepiten?*" He smiled and acted rather oddly, saying, "Yes, I am." The next day our tutor said, "Today I will teach you how to say, "I am the son of Mrs. Lepiten." It seemed I had left out a very important part of my sentence. I should have said, "*Ikaw ba ang anak nga lalaki ni Mrs. Lepiten.*" By my question I was actually asking him, "Are you the lover of Mrs. Lepiten?" The son, however,

48

realized I was just learning the language and was very gracious about it. It was important to be willing to make mistakes; that is the only way one really learns.

We also had a lot to learn about the culture. One night when there was a full moon, I heard the barking of dogs and the cry of a goat. I had noticed earlier that afternoon that a goat was tied to the fence across the street. When I looked out the window, I was horrified to see a pack of dogs trying to kill the goat so they could eat it. I put on my long robe and with my long hair flying I ran down the stairs and out the door to see if I could help the goat. I picked up stones and began throwing them at the dogs. Finally, they left.

The next day a story went around the neighborhood that a white-skinned fairy with long hair and a long robe appeared and waved her magic wand, making the dogs go away. This was only the beginning of my learning about the belief many people held in ghosts, goblins, elves, fairies, and especially evil spirits. There actually were witch doctors, to which people would go to get "medicines" and say incantations to drive away evil spirits. Often a burnt offering of a chicken was given to appease these evil spirits. How we longed to see these people released from the bondages of fear and falsehoods! (The issue of evil spirits is real, but the solution is only found in Jesus.)

After about four months, we could converse with people in Cebuano on very simple subjects. I wrote out my personal testimony of how I came to know Jesus and read it at a women's' meeting. Fred helped in a tent campaign by reading the Scriptures that went along with the filmstrip of Biblical stories. I'll never forget how hard it was for us to pronounce, *"tutoktugaok"* -- the sound that a rooster makes. It was part of the story about Peter's denial of Jesus. How amazing it was to find out that the noises animals make were spoken differently in this country, phonetically imitating the animal in question.

After about six months of study, we were asked to help out at the Bible Training School that had just started a few months before we arrived. The Director, Irv Bjelland, needed a rest, so I got to teach Christian Education, a course I had taken in College and loved. I appreciated the challenge of teaching these four young men, all older

49

than me, what a good Sunday school program would look like in the local church.

The churches were mostly small grass shelters with dirt or sand floors. But I didn't mind the setting. I just wanted the students to interact more with the Sunday school students and to get them to think. Being a neophyte, I didn't know what the educational system was like in the Philippines. I soon found out it was basically rote memorization. Often only the teacher had a book, so the students had to repeat the lesson or write it on their slates. It wasn't about understanding how to solve problems; it was about getting the right answers. So, my new ideas didn't sit well with these young men. One day one of them stood up in class and told me so! I was so humiliated that I ran in tears from the classroom. I had a lot to learn!

My job was also to teach these four men, who would become our first pastors of the churches that were being started, a little bit about music. We had an old small pump organ, so I gave each of them a private lesson each week. I would have to take an old, beat up bus with wooden seats and chickens, goats, and many other paraphernalia as my traveling companions, and travel over an unpaved, bumpy road for a half an hour to get to the Bible School. How disconcerting it was to arrive on the campus and to not be able to find even one of my piano students! Many years later I was told by these young men, who were now seasoned pastors in ministry, how they used to run and hide when they knew I was coming! Such were the joys of teaching and also learning about Philippine culture!

About two years into our first tour of duty, I began to have tremors. I saw Dr. Jack Hill, who was an American doctor in Cebu City. He made me write out my weekly schedule of activities. He was shocked when he read that I was working about 80 hours a week! He said I must go on bed rest. Rather than put me in a hospital he invited me to stay in his home with his family; this home was right next door to the Mission Guest House. He put me on a drug called Librium and I basically just ate and slept for three weeks. After two weeks he had me come to the swimming pool with his family and try swimming a little. I could barely swim. He said he would let me go back home to Bogo, three hours north of Cebu City, but suggested I not be allowed to do any ministry for six months.

With so much time on my hands, I did a lot of reading, playing the piano, and arranging flowers. Fortunately I had a house maid who did all the housework. Fred and I had been trying to have a baby for the nine years we had been married. We had even seen doctors about our problem. How thrilled we were to find out we were pregnant! I went through the usual three months of afternoon sickness, but I was so filled with joy that it was worth it all. I decided I needed to get some maternity clothes made, so I picked out material and took it to one of the local seamstresses. But I would never get to wear them.

A week after having the clothing made, I went into labor. I was rushed to the hospital in Cebu City, three hours away; but on the way, in the dark of night, I apparently miscarried. We never found the fetus. I went into another downward spiral, and grieved so deeply that the Mission finally decided to send us home on furlough six months earlier than our scheduled home leave. It was one devastation on top of another, and I just couldn't cope.

Dr. Hill recommended I see a doctor at Pine Rest Hospital in Grand Rapids, Michigan. They decided to admit me into the psychiatric ward. What an experience that was! I'll never forget the terrible feeling of being locked in! Would I ever get out again? I wasn't psychotic, just crushed and bruised from so much loss.

I stayed in that hospital for three weeks. It was interesting getting to know the other patients. The "treatment" given to many of them was electric shock, and it really seemed to reignite their lives again. I was told that some of them came back about every six months for another "shock treatment." They really didn't use "talk therapy" to help one deal with their problems. I was called three times to see the psychiatrist. He kept insisting that my problems were sexual. I couldn't see that as a problem at all! So we never got anywhere in our therapy sessions.

During this time in the hospital I got to go to various classes. One of these was a woodwork shop. This is where I made the doll cradle that I gave to Mia, my fifth grandchild, for her first birthday.

Even while we were still in the Philippines, we had been pursuing the possibility of adopting a child when we went on furlough. When I got out of the hospital, we again pursued this possibility through the PLO Adoption Agency in Detroit. We were so excited when we got a letter saying they had approved us for adoption and had a little boy for us.

However, before we could adopt the child this had to be approved by the county Judge. He said he needed time to think about it. His response was that he would only let us adopt this boy if our home would become "more stable." In other words, Fred would need to find a job in the States and we would need to stay in the States and make a "stable" home for this child.

This was another heavy blow to us. Our call to the Philippines was at stake. Did we really believe God had called us there? If so, then we would have to sacrifice our desire for this child in order to be obedient to the Lord! My dream of having a baby by Christmas was dashed to pieces! It was the saddest Christmas I ever had.

When Dr. Keith Knopf, whom we mentioned earlier in this story, heard about this great disappointment, he called us. He suggested we try adopting through the Evangelical Welfare Association in California.

We immediately contacted this agency; they asked us for pages and pages of documents. In the final analysis they said, "You can come out here to California, but we can't promise you a child; some people have been on a waiting list for two years. You would have to go through all the testing and interviews with the Social Worker just like everyone else." We decided to ask God to show us what to do. We did this by "putting out a fleece."

We were presently living in the Detroit area because my family lived there. We had bought a 24-foot house trailer to live in. It was now the dead of winter – January. But we decided if we could sell this trailer in the dead of winter without losing any money on it, perhaps God was telling us to go to California.

That is exactly what happened; a young married couple bought it for $50 more than we paid for it. By the second week of January, my Dad and I had packed up our little car with all our personal belongings. Fred had already left for the West Coast to speak in a number of churches in the Pacific Northwest, so without his knowledge I decided to drive to California by myself. I was so determined to have this child. After four days of driving I arrived at the home of Dr. Keith and Florice, who had invited me to stay with them until I could settle into an apartment.

Four days later, I had moved into an apartment just down the street from Knott's Berry Farm. By the time Fred arrived, we were ready to proceed through all the interviews, tests, and social workers visits. 10 days later we had our baby! YES! Our darling baby boy -- we named him Daniel Kevin. Daniel, meaning "God is my judge," because we wanted him to grow up to be like the Daniel in the Bible – standing strong in his faith and serving God through his family, church, work, and the Rotary Club, which he certainly has done.

How we enjoyed having this precious gift in our home! Six months later his adoption was official. By the time he was eight months old, we were back in the Philippines to begin our second term or tour of service. This time we would be sent to a new area to start a church all on our own! What joy this was to finally get to do what we had been preparing for all our lives!

Chapter 8
(1962-1968)

CHURCH PLANTING
"As you are going into all the world, preach the gospel"

After consultation with our Baptist Mission, visits to various possible places, and much prayer, we decided to settle on the other side of the mountain from Cebu City in a city called Toledo. Lest you think of this as similar to Toledo, Ohio, let me explain: This was a port city on the west coast of Cebu Island. It was an ideal place to start a church for many reasons: (1) The Christian family of Domingo Parreno was asking us to come and start a church. (2)  Even though the city was only two blocks long, it was strategic because it was a port city. (3) Two very large industries operated in this area: Atlas Consolidated Mines, the second largest open pit copper mine in the world, and the Atlas Fertilizer Plant.

 After much searching, we finally found an adequate house we could renovate for our dwelling. It was a very typical Filipino style house: thatched roof, wood siding -- the inside and outside wall were the same; we could actually see outside through the cracks! It also was built on posts about 3 feet above ground. It was made this way so the chickens, pigs, and any other smaller animals could live under the house. It had two very small bedrooms, a living room, a dining room, and a kitchen.

The mission always insisted that we had screens on our windows and indoor plumbing, so we had these things added. We also had brought with us from the States a gas operated refrigerator and wringer-type washing machine. We had brought these items with us five years earlier when we first left for the Philippines, and had left them in storage while we were abroad.

While the house was being renovated, I stayed in Cebu City with Kevin at the Mission Guest House, and this is where he learned to walk. Finally, moving day came. Our jeep and a rented truck carried all of us and our belongings over the mountain. Part of the mountain road was only one-way traffic, so we had to wait about 45 minutes for the traffic to come through from the other side. But while we waited, we enjoyed refreshments at the little *"bahay kubo"* (little hut-store). Of course everyone loved touching Kevin and playing with him while we waited. He loved all the attention! (Has anything changed?)

When we arrived in Toledo, the carpenters were still working on the renovations. Fred also decided he needed an office and a carport, so they built this on the lot next door.

Every morning before the carpenters began work, Fred would do a little teaching from the Bible and pray for them before they started. One of these carpenters was very interested, and soon wanted to become a follower of Jesus. Fred soon discovered that he was a "witch doctor"; this tradition had been passed down from his ancestors. After encountering the true source of God's power through the Holy Spirit, he was set free from these evil powers that had kept him in bondage to fear all his life. This is why we had come here! It was so great to see God already drawing people to the truth in these early months after our arrival.

Fred also decided to make friends with the local parish priest, Fr. Andres Flores, and to let him know why we were there. This encounter went very well. He even invited the priest to our house to see the movie, Martin Luther. Afterwards they had a good friendly discussion about the movie.

We tried to get involved as much as possible with community events. The yearly town fiesta was soon approaching, and they were going to have a parade. We decided to enter. We got the carpenters to help build a big box that fit over our jeep. I covered it with sheets, and we used twigs and local plants to decorate it. On the top we had a big open Bible made with big letters that said, "You shall know the truth and the truth shall set you free." We paraded our "float" through the town and won first prize! After that we took the big Bible and put it on top of our house where passers-by could see it, and it stayed there for the four years we lived there.

The next event we did was to conduct a Vacation Bible School for all the children who wanted to come. We must have had about 50 children. The Parreno's helped us teach and some of the mothers helped with the crafts. The theme of the two-week school had to do with boats and ships. At the end of the school, we had a program in which the children performed for their families and friends, singing all the songs they learned about Jesus' love and quoting Scriptures. This gave us a real opening into the community.

All of this prepared the community for the big Tent Campaign we would hold a few months later. This was the common way of starting churches in those days in our mission. This tent held about 500 people. We hired an evangelist and an assistant, Eddie Lacaba and Max Bayno, to come and help us. It was amazing to see how the Holy Spirit spoke through these men to show people how to have a personal relationship with Jesus.

This campaign continued nightly for six weeks. Each night there would be joyful singing from flip charts. Instruments would consist of an accordion, a little pump organ, or horns. Bible stories would be animated  through filmstrips -- one from the Old Testament, and one from the life of Christ. Someone would read the script while they watched the pictures flash on the screen. Once in a while we had movies. There wasn't even a movie theater in town, so we provided the only entertainment for the community. Fortunately we had borrowed a generator from the mission so we could have electricity. After the animated stories, the evangelist would preach, stressing the need for each person to receive God's precious gift of salvation by coming forward to indicate their desire to follow Jesus.

One night, Mr. Landring Bartolaba came forward; everyone was shocked! He was well known in the area as the "town drunkard". His salvation experience that night changed his life completely. He stayed sober and spent his time reading the Bible -- very slowly however, as he only had a 1st grade education. Eventually he became a Sunday school teacher for the adults, because God really gave him knowledge and wisdom. He and his beautiful wife raised 10 children. At this writing, his wife is still living, and most of his children are believers.

So back to my story -- after six weeks of tent meetings, about 50 people had come to faith in Christ, but some were uneducated. Seven of the women could not read, so I decided to teach them. Every morning they would come to the office and for two hours I would teach them how to read their own language. I used Frank Laubach's method called, "Each one, Reach one, Teach one." These women had as many as eight children and two were pregnant again, but they worked hard. By the end of three months,  they could read. Their graduation took place in front of the church; they had to read a portion of Scripture to graduate. What a joy it was for us to revisit these dear people in 2001, more than 30 years later, and to see their enduring faithfulness in the Lord and the growth of their church.

On the personal side, we were still longing to have more children. My gynecologist whom I had been seeing for a number of years, and who had discovered that my infertility was because of endometriosis, suggested I have surgery. This worked! And I was soon pregnant with our next baby!

Barbara Osbron, another missionary, loaned me a book on Natural Childbirth. I decided this was the way I wanted to have my baby. It wasn't easy, but I did it! What made it more difficult than usual was that she came out posterior, but she was beautiful. Happy, but so exhausted, I remember not being able to even brush my teeth! Mary Tillman and Barbara Espland were soon there to congratulate me and help me brush my teeth. Denise Kristine was born August 11, 1965.

Fred brought Kevin up to see his new little sister. I still get tears in my eyes when I remember how speechless he was! He just didn't know what to say or do. Finally he uncovered her and gently touched her legs and arms and kissed her forehead. It was love at first sight!

After a few days we traveled back over the mountains to our home in Toledo. We were welcomed by the whole community. The owner of our house, Mrs. Auring Trocio, immediately grabbed the baby from me, and from then on she took on the role of grandma. Another side note about her: we had shared Christ with her many times, but she was a strong Roman Catholic and big financial giver to the church. However, when we went back to Toledo City in 2001, I heard this story about her:

When Mrs. Trocio was 97 years old she found out she only had a few months to live. She called the pastor of the Baptist Church we had helped start to come and see her. She then asked him how she could know for sure she would go to heaven when she died. He opened the Scriptures and showed her the way. After that she asked Christians to come to her house daily and teach her more of the Bible; she also told her friends and relatives. The seed we had sown 35 years previously had finally bore fruit!

How I enjoyed having two children to care for! Once a week we would take them to the ocean for a picnic and paddle around in a little outrigger canoe. One time when we only took Kevin, we took the canoe out in the ocean. Suddenly strong winds blew and we  knew we must get back to the shore. We paddled fiercely, but the waves started coming into the canoe. Three-year-old Kevin was sitting in the middle, trying to help by bailing the water out of the boat. Suddenly the canoe sank. Fred and I jumped out of the canoe and Fred grabbed Kevin just as he was going under. Fortunately the water was only up to our waists.

Kevin and Denise really entertained each other. He would always watch over her and take her hand as she was learning to walk. They played outdoors a lot. The two household helpers would keep an eye on them when I was away visiting the women in the neighborhood or doing deskwork. But I could watch them out the window over my desk. One day I looked out just in time to see 20-month-old Denise trying to climb up the three steps to the door. Suddenly she missed the step and her mouth hit the step and popped out one of her baby teeth. We rushed her to the dentist, but he was unable to do anything. She was toothless in that spot until her new tooth came in when she was six.

My Doctor had told me that the endometriosis would come back once I started having my monthly periods again. She suggested I breast feed until I got pregnant with the next one, and that's exactly what happened. Denise was 22 months old when David Kim was born on June 15, 1967. He was our longest and heaviest baby. Today he is the tallest of all -- 6'4".

His birth happened like this: I had gone to Cebu City to stay at the Guest House with Kevin and Denise until David was born. Kevin had a hernia that needed repair, so we decided to have that done while we waited for David's arrival. On the third day after his surgery, as I was resting in a chair in the hospital near Kevin's bed, I began to feel contractions. Finally I called a nurse and they discovered I was very close to delivering the baby! I said, "Oh, no, I have to run home first and get my things!" They didn't want me to leave the hospital, but we checked Kevin out and took him back to the Guest House, and I grabbed my things and got back to the hospital about 6 pm. David was born at 11:30 pm. A side note on this story is that the mission gave an increase in salary when you had a child born on or before the 15th of the month. David made it just in time! Good planning, Fred!

By this time, the church numbered about 45 adults and they were able to call and support their own pastor. We had helped them buy land and begin building their church, so it was time for us to leave. When David was six weeks old, we traveled back to the USA for a one-year furlough. This time we decided to live near Bethel College in the duplex owned by the mission. I was able to take a music class at Bethel College under Dr. Berglund in choral conducting. Fred was sent out to the churches to report to them what God had been doing in our lives and ministry during the past four years. Sometimes the whole family would go with him, especially on weekends when he was speaking near home.

We lived in the duplex, which is now owned by Dick and Elenor Varberg. I remember that Denise, almost two, started her first "art work" with crayons on the newly decorated wallpaper in her bedroom! When she grew up, she became an interior designer.

One of my worries about Kevin was that he would be deficient in speaking English, as in Toledo he spoke fluent Cebuano and some Hilogaynon (Ilongo) as well. I would make him tell me things in English so he wouldn't forget his native language. I really didn't need to worry because when he got to the States, he immediately switched to English and we couldn't get him to say even one word in Cebuano!

He started kindergarten that fall. Now Denise and David enjoyed playing together while Kevin was in school. One day a week, Denise and David would go to a church day care so I could do my studying and they could have other children to play with.

During that year in the States, we often went to visit my family in Michigan and Fred's family in Racine, Wisconsin. We also went to Stanton, Michigan where my grandma, aunts, uncles, and cousins lived. Everyone got to see our lovely growing family. The children were all blessed with hugs and gifts.

By June we were getting ready to go back to the Philippines again. We had ordered a Marimba for me to take back with us; we had taken it out of the packaging and brought it into the house leaving the packaging on the floor in the garage. Kevin decided to see if it would burn. It sure did -- right under the gas tank of the car! Kevin came running into the house looking scared to death – and speechless. Fred ran down to the garage, grabbed the flaming cardboard packaging and threw it into the alley. He still has the scar on his hand from second-degree burns, but it saved the car and the garage from exploding! Sometimes being a parent is very costly. Again we saw God's hand of protection and love hovering over us.

My parents drove to Minnesota to say goodbye again before we left for another four years. It must have been hard on them, but they never complained about our going. Fred's mother had a hard time though. She couldn't understand why Fred couldn't just be a pastor somewhere here in the USA so she could see him and her grandchildren more often.

We were excited about going back "home." We already knew the direction God had for us, which we will tell you about in the next chapter.

Various means of Philippine transportation

| Typical over-crowded bus | Kevin in front of horse drawn "parada" | Canoes similar to one Kevin was capsized |

Chapter 9
(1968-1973)

SMALL BEGINNINGS
God's love gives us purpose: "Love God; love people."

All five of us -- Fred, Kevin 5½, Denise 3, 1-year-old David, and I -- arrived in Cebu City for our third term. We found a lovely American-type, ranch-style house just perfect for our growing family. The only renovation we had to do was paint! What a blessing! We were eager to get settled in our own place. We had shipped a couple of barrels of needed items for the family for the next four years.

The Baptist General Conference had a mission depot of all new things where we could go and pick up whatever we needed for free. I "shopped" there for clothing for the children for the next four years. I could also get kitchenware and linens, as well as toys for the children. Christmas at our house was getting into the barrels and bringing out the items the kids would like for Christmas.

Our barrels arrived about a month after we did, and I began the process of going through them. One day, I had gotten to the bottom of one barrel and found that my precious black pepper had broken open; it was causing me to sneeze profusely. Then I began feeling sick to my stomach, but it didn't take long to realize that this was "morning sickness."

Yes, I was pregnant again! Our fourth child arrived seven months later -- a darling little boy that looked a lot like Fred. First we named him Donovan Kirk, but on the fourth day of his birth we changed his name to Daran Kris. This name just fit him better. He was born on May 15th 1969. Fred did it again! (Got another increase in pay!)

We were very thankful for the great education our children got at the Cebu International School. School started in July: Kevin was now in 1st grade and Denise was starting kindergarten. I'll never forget the first drawing she brought home from school. The assignment was to draw a picture of a person. Denise was two months away from being four years old. I thought this was quite ambitious for such a young child. I wish I had kept the drawing -- just a big head with eyes and a mouth and a little hair! I think she was the youngest one in the class. Both the children loved school and made a lot of friends. David, meanwhile, now had Daran as a playmate at home.

After two years into our third term, we decided to move to a brand new bungalow on Busay hill. This house was built into the hill, so there was a walk-out basement. This was developed into a soundproof recording studio for Fred's ministry. Here daily programs were produced to be aired on the local stations.

We all loved this new house up on a hill overlooking Cebu City. The children now had a lot more room to explore and play. About this same time, we got a German shepherd dog. After we bred her she produced eight puppies. What fun our children had playing with these puppies. We did sell all of them eventually, but we kept Chubby, the mother, who was a great friend for the children as well as a good watchdog.

The lot next door to our house was empty and made an excellent playground for the children, but the fence on the back side had not yet been built. There was a drop-off of about seven feet to a cement pad below. One day, Kevin and Denise were playing there when Denise fell off the cliff onto the cement pad and landed on her head. I heard her scream and ran to see what happened. I was horrified and very scared. I picked her up and carried her inside. She began to vomit; I realized how serious this was, so I put her in the car and drove to the doctor's office. There was no 911 to call! The elevator was broken so I carried her up two flights of stairs; she was seven years old at this time so this wasn't a light load to carry! But of course I never even thought about how heavy she was, only about the results of the fall.

The doctor immediately told me to take her to the hospital. The doctor soon diagnosed her with a concussion. Just a hair length away and she would have had a fracture. She developed fluid between her brain and her skull; this was really scary. We could touch her skull and feel how soft it was! If this swelling didn't go down by the next day they were going to have to go in and drain the fluid. We never prayed so hard in our whole lives; we also asked our colleagues and fellow believers to pray as well. God was so good to us even in our foolishness for not having that fence finished before allowing the children back there. He healed our darling seven year old! We learned a great lesson from that experience. We really needed a parenting book!

Fred had a motor scooter as this time, and he would take the kids, usually two at a time, on rides up in the hills beyond our house. Up the hill was the garden of the Carmelite Sisters' Convent filled with beautiful plants and statues. We hardly ever saw the Sisters because they lived in recluse, but the children loved to go for walks up there. I remember especially when all the other children were in school, Daran would often ask "Mommy, can we go see Jesus?"

While still living in Toledo during our previous term, Hartley Christenson, a missionary working just an hour north of us, and Fred decided to try producing radio programs. Finding a place to do this that was quiet was quite a challenge. They ended up recording in a little abandoned chicken coop far away from a housing area. But they still had rooster crowing sounds on their recordings.

The purpose of making these recordings and putting them on radio stations was to try to reach people who lived in remote areas with God's message. Voice of Truth became the name of the program. Each segment would also invite people to write in for a free Bible correspondence course. This became a very effective avenue of evangelism.

It had been two years now since these radio programs had been started. The Mission saw how effective this was and felt that Fred should be the one to develop Mass Media further. Soon Fred was producing a wide range of daily programming on 14 different radio stations. These were being produced in the Cebuano dialect, for use on commercial stations. On weekends the programs were in English, targeting the youth.

Original International School of Cebu

Pay attention Daran

Climbing a coconut tree

Fred Motorcycle (1971)
David, Daran & Denise

Fred utilized the preaching skills of our Cebuano pastors and evangelists for making good radio programs, so until a major recording studio was built they would come to our little studio under the house to record day after day.

 Suddenly, one afternoon there was an earthquake strong enough to topple bookcases in the radio-recording studio under the house! The children and I ran outside and huddled together under a big tree. Fred happened to be in the studio at the time and was able to hold the recording equipment from toppling over. Very little damage resulted. Again we experienced God's protection over us. He is SO GOOD to His children!

In December of 1971, my father, Glenn Jones, came to spend a month with us. This was such a treat! Our children hardly knew their grandparents, as they only got to see them every four years. Dad thoroughly enjoyed his time there; in his memoirs he wrote that this was a real highlight in his life. He got involved with Fred's ministry, preaching and teaching whenever he could. He had always wanted to be a missionary and he saw his desire fulfilled, even though it was only for a month.

While Fred was busy with Mass Media, I got more involved at the International School our children were attending. I offered to work with the music program and started a 4th to 7th grade choir. Kevin got to participate in this. Through this avenue, I became better acquainted with the school and the teachers. I decided to get permission to start a Bible Club after school for anyone who wanted to attend. Besides teaching the children the Word of God and having them memorize verses, we had singing and crafts. The class grew very rapidly and I looked around for some help.

Just about this time, Bonnie Barrows, daughter of the famous Cliff Barrows with the Billy Graham Association, came to live next door to us. Her grandparents were living there while they worked with the Gideons, placing Bibles in the schools, hotels and businesses. Bonnie became almost a part of our family. She loved to come over and play with the children. I'm sure they all have fond memories of her. I asked her if she would help me with the children's Bible Club, and she jumped at the opportunity! The following year, she also started a Bible Study with the teachers at the International School.

One of the great rewards from this was the response of the assistant principal. The Bible Study sent her on a new road, seeking to learn all she could about God and His love for her. Eventually she made the decision to follow Him with her whole heart. Her joy was so evident to everyone. Presently she is the Principal of Bethel International School (started by Paul Varberg), which now has about 400 students and is located in Tacloban City, Leyte. God knew this school would need a wonderful, well-trained Principal who followed Jesus. He opened her eyes to the truth, changed her life, and filled her with His Holy Spirit, thus preparing her for a ministry in this school.

Soon it was time for furlough again. This time we decided to return to the States through Israel and Europe. The Harvey Espland family decided to go with us. Our children were 3, 5, 7, and 9. Theirs were 14 and 11. We had a fun time seeing all the sites where Jesus lived and taught. Then we went to Paris. Most of the time, Doug Espland would have Daran on his shoulders. At the Paris airport I found Doug, but no Daran! We started running back toward the terminal and then I saw him; he was happily licking an ice cream cone with a security guard at his side talking to him in French. God was watching over him even when I wasn't!

We parted ways with the Esplands in Paris, rented a car and traveled for two more weeks in Europe. I think the place the children liked the most was Salzburg, Austria where the story of "The Sound of Music" took place. We stayed at an inn that had a barn right next to it. The children got to go in the barn and see a newly born calf.

Another fun time in this area was visiting the historic home of a former bishop of Hellbrunn Palace near Salzburg, who loved to play practical jokes on his guests. He developed a water system that would spray his guests when he pressed a secret button. He would seat his guests in the garden around a stone table on stone chairs, which had a hole in the middle of the seat. The guests were only allowed to stand up if the Bishop stood up. His joke on them was to push a button that made water squirt up on all the seats. Since it was improper for them to stand up to avoid the water, they just had to sit there and endure getting wet!

As we toured each of the scenes where water was used to move the manikins, the tour guide would push a button and people in our tour group would get wet. Kevin watched carefully and discovered where the buttons were. So at one point, he slyly moved over to it and, when the tour guide was not looking, pushed the button and got the tour guide wet! I think that was the beginning of Kevin's love for playing jokes on others.

We also toured along the Rhine River, seeing many of the castles in Germany. We took the ferry across the straights to England -- seeing the famous "Cliffs of Dover" on the way. We rented a third floor "Zimmer-frie" (guest house) in a town along the coast for three days. The owners of the home loved our children and took them ice-skating for the first time.

The hardest thing about traveling with children ages 3, 5, 7, and 9 in foreign countries was finding food they would eat. Often we had to settle for plain rice, bread, eggs, and cheese. When we finally got to Amsterdam, the kids spotted a McDonald's a block away and ran as fast as they could to it. They had quite a feast that day.

In Amsterdam, we saw Ann Frank's house, where she and her family hid many years during the World War II when Ann was about 12-14 years old. She wrote in her diary every day. This has been put into a book and also made into a movie. Just before the war ended the Frank family was discovered and they all were killed.

One of the fun things to do in Amsterdam was to take a boat tour on the many canals – there were probably more canals than roads in Amsterdam. This is the best way to really see the city.

We spent our year on furlough in Royal Oak, Michigan -- very close to the church that had ordained Fred and sent us out as missionaries. The church fixed up a little home for us to stay in and supplied us with everything we needed. We had a big empty lot next door, which became a wonderful place for the children to play. Fred immediately went out and bought a couple of bicycles for the kids. It didn't take long before Kevin, Denise, and David had learned how to ride. Daran, only 3, decided he was going to learn how to ride as well. With just a couple of pushes he was soon balancing and keeping up with the older children.

In the winter, we taught the kids how to make igloos and snowmen. They had a great time since they hadn't seen snow for four years. One day, when the older three were in school, Daran took a bucket and shovel out in the snow to play. Soon he filled up his bucket and brought the snow in the house; he told me he wanted to keep it. I decided to let him discover what would happen. After his nap he went to see his "snow" which was now water, of course. He cried because all his snow had melted, so I gave him a little science lesson that day.

My mother needed a place to live, so Fred gave up his little office behind the kitchen and she moved in. She wasn't there very often, as she worked long hours at a department store. Sometimes she would babysit for us as well. Dad was so generous and paid my way down to Florida to spend a week with him. My parents were now divorced, so it was hard to have Dad over for a visit. I know he missed this very much.

One of the fun things I did was take Jazz lessons on the piano from my brother, Nate. He gave me a lesson every week in exchange for a meal. It was fun, but being a classical player, learning jazz was a big stretch for me. I needed to see the notes! I never really got the hang of it, but it was fun just having this time with my youngest brother, 13 years younger than me.

A couple of months before we returned to the Philippines, our church choir performed an Easter Concert. They asked me to sing one stanza of the song, "So Send I You." I was going through a personal struggle at this time about going back again to the Philippines. With my parents divorcing, I felt I was needed by my family. So as I sang the solo at church, the words of the song began to touch me deeply. I actually broke down and cried; I had to once again surrender myself to God's will, not my will. BUT -- I was about to learn a great lesson: YOU JUST CAN'T OUTGIVE GOD!

Chapter 10
(1973 -1977)

AMAZING YEARS
"Behold the day is coming, says the Lord, when I will pour out my spirit on all flesh."

Of all the times we left the USA for the Philippines, this was definitely the hardest. I felt that my five siblings, though 18 years old and above, still needed their oldest sister around. But I just had to leave them in God's hands and go with my husband back to Cebu City. God had given me a wonderful Scripture: "I have become all things to all people so that I might win some" (1 Corinthians 9:22). I chose this to be my life verse from that time on. Just how this would play out in my life was yet to be seen.

We immediately found a house to live in. It was the house just behind that of Jerry and Barbara Osbron. We had known them for many years, and had even worked with them at Bethany Baptist Church in St. Paul, MN in the youth program when we first got married. They had four children also, some of them the same ages as ours. The school was only a short walk from our house; it was an ideal place to live. This marked the first time we had a two-story house for a living space, so the children had plenty of room. We got our dog, Chubby, back too. The children all seemed to love being "back home" again.

Furloughs can be difficult for missionary children, having to adjust to American ways, and making friends only to have to leave them after one year. Many missionaries no longer follow this plan and have found other creative ways to teach the children while in their home country, like home schooling. This way they are also free to travel with their father when he speaks at different churches. Some missionaries also take more frequent and shorter furloughs, just for the summers.

Since Fred was now working full-time in Mass Media, he was asked to oversee the construction of an office building and radio-recording studio. He also started writing a daily devotional called "Moment of Truth," published in each of the four newspapers in Cebu City. Next Fred got the idea of having a "Dial-a -Devotion" on the telephone -- the first of its kind as far as we know, at least in the Philippines. This became very popular in Cebu. People would be calling all day long. One man said he had to call at midnight because he couldn't get through any other time, as there was only one phone line. People could listen to a one-minute inspirational word when they called, but they could not respond; it was simply a service to the public.

What happened next was another great advancement in Mass Media. One day Fred got a call from a Catholic priest who had been reading Fred's newspaper articles. The priest said he co-hosted a TV show every Wednesday where the people's problems were discussed utilizing community people who were skilled in those areas. He asked Fred if he would be willing to be on the panel to discuss youth problems on his show. Fred was delighted to have this opportunity; the mission agreed that this was a great opportunity as well.

The morning after Fred was on this TV show, he got a call from the station manager who said, "I saw you on the show last night, and I liked what you had to say. I am wondering if you would like to have your own TV show." Fred immediately thanked him, but said he didn't have the financial backing for that. The station manager countered, "How about if I give you an hour every Sunday afternoon for free?"

God had much bigger plans for us than just a radio ministry. Fred was being stretched in having to produce weekly, one-hour TV programs as well. Sometimes he used the Moody Science series and other good Christian movies, including those produced by World Wide Pictures (Billy Graham); other times he interviewed famous people passing through the city. I tried to help him as much as I could with music. Once in a while I would even direct the show! Fred even took a specialized TV production course while on home leave, as well radio and television production classes at the University of Minnesota.

71

One Christmas, I decided to produce a Christmas song for the telecast, "Jesus, our Brother, Kind and Good." I used some of our children as well as the Buot children. The Buots' were very close friends of ours who also had four children about the ages of our children. This was exciting for me as I could use my gifts in acting and music.

Many interesting things happened the two years we lived in this house. A very unfortunate accident happened to David when he was 8 years old. He slammed the door on his finger so hard that it cut off the tip of his fore finger at the bottom of the fingernail. This happened just before guests were arriving for a surprise birthday party for Fred. We rushed David to the hospital. The doctor asked if we had brought the cut off part of the finger. We said, "No!" He said he might be able to reattach it if he had it. We called our home and one of the guests, Moya Jackson, a British lady, was there and we asked her to please run upstairs and see if she could find the finger. She was horrified, as she hated bloody things, but she and her husband brought the fingertip to the hospital.

The doctor tried to attach it, but it was too late, so the surgeon cut a piece from under David's arm to cover his finger. This surgeon, we found out, had just arrived the week before from the USA. His specialty was HAND surgeries! Again our God provided just what we needed! He is an awesome God.

The next big event that I remember was the Ralph Bell Crusade, sponsored by the Billy Graham Evangelistic Association. Fred and I got very involved in helping with this. Hundreds of people came to Christ during these weeks at the stadium in Cebu City. Our reward was to discover that our fifth child had been conceived!

We waited until our vacation time in May in Baguio to tell the children. I really don't remember exactly how we told them, but their story is that we asked them if they would like a puppy or a new baby in the family. They voted for a puppy! Now it could be they just say this to tease their little sister. We welcomed Deborah Karin into our family November 27, 1974. Let me tell you about her birth.

In those days there were no ultrasounds in Cebu City, so we couldn't find out whether we were having a boy or a girl. I just decided that it would probably be another boy, although secretly I would have loved to have a girl so that Denise could have a sister.

I was 40 years old at this time. Debi was 10 days overdue, so the doctor decided to induce labor. The labor was only three hours long, but very intense. I remember my dear friend, Tita Buot came to encourage me; she had been pregnant with her fifth, but had a miscarriage. This must have been very hard for her to see me having my baby. She put my needs ahead of hers. That's what real friends do!

When Debi was born, I just couldn't believe that it was a girl! I cried with joy saying, "Oh God, you are SO GOOD to me for giving me the deep desire of my heart".

Dedication Daran & Debi

We could tell Debi was "overdue"; her body was covered with scaly skin that was peeling off, but it didn't take long for this to go away. She had dark hair and beautiful dark eyes like her father. We all enjoyed having her join our family, although I found out years later that Daran, who was just 5½, was a bit jealous. Perhaps he felt like he was being replaced. He was also now going to school all day, so baby sister got to spend all day with Mom. For the past two years he had been home alone with Mom, going and doing everything she did. He especially loved grocery shopping; even to this day he loves to shop for groceries, take them home, and use his skills to cook fabulous gourmet meals.

I really loved being a Mom at 40! Sometimes people who did not know me would stop to admire little Debi, and exclaim how beautiful my grandchild was. How embarrassed they were when I told them I was her mother!

One day while I was shopping in downtown Cebu City, I had a strong urge to stop at the Christian Book Store even though it was raining hard. I really had nothing to buy there, but I found out God had a purpose. There was only one customer in the store; she was very pregnant and crying. I started a conversation with her and found out she was destitute. The father of her child, a serviceman, had gone back to the States and she now had no means of support for her other three children.

This began a ministry to Nenita for the next few years. We immediately went shopping for food and I kept praying about how best to help her. I took her to her house -- just a little *nipa* house on the public land next to the cemetery. I inquired what she had that she could sell. Then I asked her what skills she had, and found out she knew how to do manicures and pedicures. I really believe in helping people, though not just giving handouts, but hand-ups. I worked out a little business for her. She came to my house and the houses of many of my friends to do manicures and pedicures each week. Of course, she had to bring all the children, whom we fed as well, but at least she was doing what she could.

Then I found out she knew how to do a very special kind of beadwork using four needles. My Grandma Jones now got involved. I would send these beaded necklaces and bracelets to her and she would sell them to her friends. Grandma also sold these at county fairs. Nenita came to know the Lord and was baptized along with 11-year-old Brenda, her eldest child, after a few months of going to church with us.

Nenita was able to at least feed her family, but then tragedy struck. When her cervical cancer was discovered, it was already way beyond surgery. They decided to give her radiation treatments. We were able to raise the money from friends in the USA to pay for these treatments. Nenita stayed in a government hospital ward so there was no hospital cost, but medications and radiation had to be paid for.

She hit her lowest point when her weight dropped to 68 lbs. Fred and I prayed for her healing, but, I must admit, not with much faith. All the other women who were getting radiation for cervical cancer had died. But God again heard the cries of His hurting child, and she lived another 31 years!

Brenda, the eldest of Nenita's children, was a very beautiful child, and one day she was discovered by a movie company. She got an audition, and eventually the company moved the whole family to Manila. Brenda became a movie star. She played in 19 movies and was cover girl on a popular magazine. She finally gave up the business when she was 19. In later years I visited her and the family in Manila; they had become very wealthy with servants and cars! Wow! Again God showed His awesome power to care for his children. After her mother died, Brenda came to visit me in California in 2003.

When the Osbrons went to the States on furlough, a house opened up for us further out of town near a small airport. We decided to move there. The children loved the big yard in the front and back of the house. We now had rabbits, dogs, and cats. We lived there until Debi was 2½. One day a friend brought her a little duckling; the duckling thought Debi was its mother and would follow her everywhere – even all over the house. Debi was also given a little chick, but unfortunately it got loved to death.

Soon after we moved to this house, Kevin got very ill and was put in the hospital with Hemorrhagic Fever. I was still nursing Debi, so I would run between the hospital and home. Fred was gone, as he had to make a trip to another island to look at the possibility of sending missionaries there. He was interim director of the Mission at that time. He wasn't feeling well when he got on the ferryboat for the overnight trip, and perhaps his illness grew worse from sleeping on one of the cots on the deck; these cots were very "up close and personal" to each other. He began to feel even worse by the time he arrived the next morning in Ormoc City, Leyte.

Fred was hoping to get a room at the only hotel in town, but it was completely booked; he could only lie down on a sofa in the 8x8 lounge for a few hours. He forced himself to get up and look around town to check out possible sites to build a church. He came back to the hotel and rested until the launch would leave at midnight to go back to Cebu. He had such a high fever that he couldn't even walk by himself to the boat. The hotel sent some staff with him to help him get on the launch. By the time he arrived in Cebu, his fever had broken and he was feeling a little better.

75

It was while he was gone that Kevin was hospitalized, so when Fred arrived, he immediately relieved me from "double" duty and stayed with Kevin overnight in the hospital. In those days in the Philippines, all patients were required to have someone stay with them.

When Fred awoke the next morning he could not talk; he had lost his voice. For a long time he had been longing to have a TV program on the only color TV channel in the city. He was finally offered time on Sunday evenings on channel 3. This was the night the first program was to begin. Fred had invited a Bible School choir from Manila to give a concert that night. The concert and telecast went on without him, as he had to stay at home, and he had to cancel his contract, not knowing when or if he would ever get his voice back. The doctors said he had a 50% chance of voice recovery.

The Mission sent him to the mountains for three weeks to recuperate. It was there in the mountains that Fred really began to seek the Lord, giving up all his personal ambitions and putting his future in God's hands. When Fred got back he was a new person spiritually; God had done a deep work in his heart. He went back to work, but he had to use a magic slate to give instructions to his staff, as he still could not talk above a whisper. But three months later, his voice returned! Just another blessing from our awesome God!

About a year before Fred's experience, I came to a real crisis in my life as well. I was just tired of living this way. God seemed far away, and reading the Bible and praying was just a bore. Another missionary, Nancy Anderson, felt a need to start praying for me. She had come back from furlough a completely changed lady -- so joyful and full of love for Jesus and other people. She loved God's Word and would always call me when she came to Cebu City. She and her husband taught at our Bible College three hours north of the city. She would read to me what God was saying to her from His Word. At first I was very defensive; after all, who was she to tell me? She was younger than me and I was a Bible teacher! But, little by little, I couldn't wait until she came to town so we could study God's Word together and pray. Another thing that was so awesome about her was the way she prayed -- she talked to God and worshipped him with such a fervent spirit! I began to pray and ask God to give me what Nancy had.

One night, when Fred was away and the children were tucked into bed, I went to my bedroom and closed the door saying, "Dear God, I'm not leaving here until you do something in my life -- please change me!" Up to this time I had been taking a drug called Librium; my whole body would shake without it. As I cried out to God He began showing me my life of bitterness and unforgiveness. It was like I was watching my life on a TV screen. God revealed things to me I had completely forgotten, but had just stuffed away. All that stuffing was now surfacing. I felt God asking me to forgive each person who had hurt me. After much crying and forgiving, I suddenly felt free! FREEDOM! I didn't even remember what that was like! I never needed to take another tranquilizer after that night!

Now I loved the Word of God! I had been given new eyes to see deeper truths. One night about four months later, while I was in prayer, I felt the presence of the Holy Spirit in a very overwhelming way. I wanted to give Jesus a special sacrificial gift. Everything we had as a couple belonged to both of us. I suddenly remembered I had a birthday coming soon and often I would get money from family in the States for my birthday -- usually $20 or $30. I was overjoyed when I realized I could give all the money I got this year to the Lord! Soon I received $70!

Then God poured out His Holy Spirit on me, and I began to worship Him in another language! What a euphoric experience! From that time on, every time I would begin to worship God that other language would come out of my mouth. What joy! But what happened to me was of greater importance; I felt more empowered to share Christ with others with more fervent compassion. God gave me boldness, joy, love, and peace!

For the next few years, it was like I was on a honeymoon with Jesus. I spent hours in worship with Him and the Bible really came alive to me. In fact, without my saying a word, everyone could see the difference. My whole countenance had changed. People would ask, "What happened to Ruth?" Some call this the Baptism of the Holy Spirit; others call it Salvation; others call it being filled with the Holy

Spirit. I really don't care what one calls it, but it is very real and available to anyone who seeks the Lord with her or his whole heart. At first, I had trouble accepting this experience as it was outside my doctrinal understanding of Scripture, but my Dad had given me a helpful book called, "They Found the Secret" by Dr. V. Raymond Edman. These are stories about great evangelists like D.L. Moody and Billy Graham. The secret they found and experienced was similar to mine! They received a deeper love for God's Word and an empowering of the Holy Spirit to evangelize or just to simply share the gospel with anyone who will listen. This confirmed to me that God sometimes works far beyond what we may think is correct doctrine to get us "out of our boxes."

Now let me tell you about the $70 I gave to the Lord. I didn't know where He wanted me to give it, so I just kept it in the bank. Then one day, a big need came to one of the members of the Bible study group I was teaching. Her husband had left her, and she had no way to pay her daughter's tuition for schooling that year. I felt I was supposed to give her this money -- it turned out to be exactly the amount she needed! I was so thrilled! It just doesn't get any better than this, I thought, but God still had so much more to show me of His love.

Each day I would drive the children to and from school. On the way home, we would often stop and buy burnt corn on the cob for a snack. One day I noticed a blind lady selling rabbits for eating. I wanted to help the poor lady, so I bought one. The children seemed to love it, thinking it was fried chicken, so I would buy one every week – that is, until one day Kevin realized the "chicken" had four drumsticks! That was the end of our eating rabbit. To the children, rabbits were pets, and you don't eat pets!

We started picking up this blind lady, Delores, and taking her to church with us. Then she would come home with us for dinner. At this time we also had a 7th grade girl staying with us while her parents were teaching at our Bible School about three hours away. She was boarding with us so she could go to school with our children. Unfortunately, unbeknown to us, Delores had lice. She had taken a nap on our sofa and the lice quickly infected all the children. The only way to get rid of it was to shampoo each head with kerosene and shampoo mix, and then to wrap each head with a towel for four hours before shampooing again. Wash all the sheets, and repeat the process again in four days. What fun! We finally got rid of the lice.

This was the year we sent Kevin off to Faith Academy in Manila to stay in a dorm for his 8th grade schooling. It was so hard to see him go, but we felt it was best for his education and sports. He became an excellent wrestler and soccer player. He adjusted very well to this big change in his life. Recently, I found a folder of all his letters he wrote to us while at school. What struck me about them was how positive they were! He always saw the best in change and adjusted accordingly.

Denise was now in sixth grade and quite a beauty; I was so shocked on Valentine's Day when a beautiful Mercedes Benz stopped in front of our house. The driver, dressed in a white uniform, went around and opened the door for a German classmate of Denise's. He had brought her a box of candy! It finally dawned on me that our little girl was becoming quite a young lady! I kept closer watch over her after that.

We really loved the school our children attended. They learned a lot about Philippine culture. About half the children were foreigners and the other half Filipinos, but everyone was required to speak English on the campus. All the children except Debi had a chance to be in plays and musicals. We always enjoyed going to their programs.

I also got involved with community activities. Because Fred was a Rotarian, I was a Rotary Ann, so I got to know some of the wealthy women of the city and had chances to minister to them. One time, I was asked to pray over the President of the club who had cancer. God didn't heal her, but I believe her faith in God became more real and that I will see her in heaven some day.

I also joined the Cebu Workshop, which was a group of foreign women who got together to help the community. We raised money for scholarships for worthy students. One of the ways was to have a walkathon. I helped by going to businesses and getting the owners to donate money for each mile we walked. I later heard that we raised more money for scholarships that year than ever before.

It was at one of these meetings that I met Val Loskota, an American whose husband was studying medicine at one of the universities in the city. She and I became good friends, and she and Bill became strong members of the little church we had started. We had a lot in common because she was about to give birth, and Debi was about a year old. Fred had the privilege of dedicating their new baby to the Lord at a family camp we had for all the church community.

Val had a beautiful voice and often sang in our church services. Two different times, she choreographed ballet dances for 11-year-old Denise. While Val sang "The Lord's Prayer" and the "Magnificat," Denise gracefully portrayed the songs in dance. This enhanced our worship immensely.

This church had started in our home on Friday nights from people who came to study the Bible. It grew rapidly, and we realized we needed help. We asked a student from our Bible School, Jerry Estacion, to make the three-hour bus ride from the school each weekend to help us start this church. He would play his guitar and lead worship as well as work with the youth. God brought a really neat group of people together. One was the dean of the Southwestern University, together with his family of seven children. Because of the TV ministry, we were beginning to reach more of the upper social strata of people in the Cebu City, which was the second largest city in the Philippines.

Eventually we moved into the upstairs of our Mass Media building. We, along with Jerry, developed this growing group into a church. When we left for the States two years later, they were able to call a pastor, Rev. Gonzalo Olojan. Later, Rev. and Mrs. Landry Tenerife became the pastors. At this writing, Landry is still the pastor of the church. Jerry continued to minister there also until he married Zeny and later brought his family to the USA.

Our last Sunday there before furlough, we all went to the beach and Fred baptized about 25 people who had become members of the Lahug Community Church. It was our privilege to visit some of these dear saints in December 2009. What a blessing to hear their stories of God working in their lives! One man, the assistant pastor of the Lahug Church, made a special effort to visit us just to thank us for bringing his father to Christ -- what a difference it has made in the next generations!

These spiritual experiences we had those past four years changed our lives and the direction of our lives forever. The next chapter of our lives took us to unchartered waters. If we had stayed in the States, we may have missed seeing God's mighty work in our lives and His precious blessings that we had yet to experience.

We left the next week with Wendell, Nancy, Scott, and Dawn Anderson for another furlough. This time we traveled through Israel and Europe. But I'll tell you about this amazing trip in the next chapter.

Chapter 11
(1977-79)

FURLOUGH – HIGHS AND LOWS
"Trials come only to make us strong"

We left Cebu for furlough in May of 1977 with our family of seven: Kevin (13), Denise (11), David (9), Daran (7), and Debi (2½), along with the Anderson Family -- Wendell, Nancy, Dawn (12), and Scott (10). We had decided to travel again through Europe. We stopped first in Greece, and then in the Holy Land. But getting into Israel was a bit of a problem for Fred!

On the plane between Athens and Tel Aviv we couldn't all sit together, so Fred ended up sitting next to an American young lady on her way to join her husband at a kibbutz, and had an opportunity to share Christ with her. As we were about to disembark, Fred took the time to get a pamphlet out of his briefcase and talk to the lady a little longer. In the meantime, the Andersons and I, along with the seven children, disembarked and got on the bus to the terminal.

There was a lot of unrest in the country because of the upcoming celebration of the 1968 victory in the Six-Day War, so the planes were parking about a mile from the terminal building because of the fear of terrorism. Apparently Fred was targeted as a suspect along with two other men on the plane; one was an Egyptian and the other a Nigerian. Fred got on the bus and stood behind me, but a security guard tapped him on the shoulder and told him to come with her. Fred said he would like to stay on this bus to be with his family. The guard left, but came back with a male guard who made it VERY CLEAR that Fred must come with him.

Fred was taken to a little paddy wagon under the wing of the plane along with the other two suspects. David, fearing for his dad, went along with them. They were each interrogated for about half an hour.

82

One question they repeatedly asked Fred was why he had returned *again* to Israel; so they really had a record on him!

In the meantime, we all waited at the terminal. About an hour later Fred was released and had caught up with us.

We returned to the same place we had stayed four years earlier -- the Casa Nova (Night House), operated by a Franciscan priest, Father Machine. He had heard we were coming. When he saw us walking up the street carrying our 17 pieces of luggage, he ran toward us with a big grin and warm words of welcome in Italian. He immediately picked up 2½-year-old Debi in his big, loving arms. What a change in this man from five years before! We soon found out that he, too, had received the Baptism (or empowering) of the Holy Spirit that was happening throughout the Roman Catholic Church at that time.

This guest house wasn't fancy, but it was clean and very loving. Each meal, we sat at long tables with all the other guests, many of whom were priests and nuns. I told Nancy, "Let's watch for some nuns we can talk to." Soon we introduced ourselves to two of them; we were delighted when they invited us to a prayer meeting that night.

What an amazing prayer meeting! We had never experienced anything like it! As people worshipped, some had their hands raised in adoration to the Lord; others were dancing before the Lord while others were on their knees. Many were quietly "praying in tongues." We felt very much at home and heartily joined in. What joy filled our hearts to finally have the freedom to worship with our whole beings! (Psalm 35:10)

We stayed at the Casanova for a week, rented a van, and did our own tour. Each day the guest house would pack us a lunch, and we would travel all over the country to "walk where Jesus walked."

En route to Israel, we stopped over in Greece for a couple of days. The children enjoyed climbing up on the ruins of the Parthenon, which was built in 447 BC. (Today climbing is no longer allowed.)

After leaving Israel, we went to Darmstadt, Germany and stayed at the guest house on the beautiful grounds of the Evangelical

Sisterhood of Mary. These sisters treated all of us like royalty. Candies were on our beds each night when we came back to our rooms. The three boys were taken by the "brothers" to the garden and allowed to help with the gardening. At each meal there would be a "sister" with us; she would not eat with us, but she would tell us fascinating stories of what God had done at the Sisterhood of Mary. Mother Basilica Schlock started this group when all the homes of her Bible Study group were destroyed during WWII. There are many books written about this group if you want to know more. After this we parted ways with the Andersons.

Our family had all planned to drive to Berlin the next day, about 8 hours away, but Kevin came down with a virus. All of us stayed with Kevin except Daran; he got to go with Fred to Berlin.

In Berlin they visited a young lady Fred had led to the Lord in Cebu City. She had responded to the message Fred preached on a morning TV show, and God used this to convict her of many sins, including abortions. A year later he had the privilege of marrying her to her German pen pal, who had also become a believer because of her testimony. When she and her husband knew we were visiting Germany, they asked Fred if he would come to Berlin and preach in their church. The following day, this couple took Fred and Daran into Eastern Europe. Who could have guessed that ten years later the wall between the East and West would be torn down? This couple sent us a piece of that wall, which we have displayed in our office.

We did some other touring around Germany, and also made a quick revisit to Amsterdam. From there we flew to Norfolk, VA, and were met by the Thomas' relatives, Fred's biological father's family. None of the children had ever met them, so this was a great celebration for all.

When we arrived in Detroit, my father was there to meet us. He was going through a very hard time as my mother was divorcing him. He went with us to Center Lake Bible Camp where Fred was the missionary speaker for the week. He was so happy to see all of us again. He asked if he could take David, who was 10 at this time, home with him by letting him ride on the back of his motor bike; he just lived a few hours away. We thought this would be a great chance for David to get to know his grandpa. How right we were!

On the way, a big storm came and Grandpa and David had to find a dry place to stay until the storm blew over. They found an old barn and hung out there for an hour or so, which gave them a chance to talk. Grandpa taught archery at the Bible Camp, so he mentioned one of the students as being a girl. David said, "How do you know it was a girl?" Grandpa said, "Because she has breasts." According to David, that was the first time he realized the difference! (Story used by permission.) Because of the conversations David had that day with Grandpa, he later prayed with us to become a follower of Jesus.

Today, David is a Civil Engineer. He worked for Cal Trans designing and redesigning roads and freeways for 15 years, and then worked five years for Parsons. At this writing, he has returned to government employment with the Riverside County Authority to have more time with his family, even though he had to take a big cut in salary. But another great plus is that he gets to head up the 91 freeway project that he and his team redesigned under the Parsons' Company.

David is also very active in short-term missions and in discipling men in his church. He is greatly respected in the workplace for his abilities and his integrity. He seeks to be God's ambassador wherever he goes. He has a very supportive wife, Lyndi, who is a fabulous cook, and two teenage children, Ian and Jacqueline.

We spent this furlough in California. Fred was asked to be the Missionary-in-residence pastor for the year at the First Baptist Church of Lakewood. This church was one of 17 special interest churches that supported us. They rented a cute little bungalow in Long Beach, and Florice Knopf was the one who helped furnish and decorate this house for us. As mentioned earlier, Dr. Keith and Florice Knopf have been our faithful friends since we first met them in 1958. Their home was always a guest home for missionaries coming and going to and from mission fields. They were very generous people as well, and always supplied missionaries with tickets to Disneyland every time they came back to the USA. Kevin and Robin have continued this practice by supplying Disneyland tickets to missionaries they support when they come on furlough.

Our small three-bedroom house with one bathroom was a little crowded for the seven of us, so Fred decided that Kevin, who was now 14, needed his own bedroom. He got permission to turn the garage into a bedroom. He had to cut through an 8" hollow block wall to make a doorway from the other bedroom into the garage. I got a great picture of Fred covered from head to toe with white cement after cutting through the wall. But it was worth it for Kevin to have his own space -- every teenager needs that! We bought a little space heater to keep him warm in the winter. Debi and Denise shared a bedroom on the other side of the bathroom, and David and Daran shared a bedroom next to Kevin's.

I remember it being a difficult year for the school-age children. Kevin and Denise went to a nearby middle school, but it was hard making friends in this "strange American culture." Denise would often complain of stomachaches and stay home from school, but she did try to get involved by joining the school choir and seemed to really enjoy it. Kevin found his niche by joining the soccer team.

At this time David, whom we were calling Kim (his middle name), got teased at school for having a "girl's" name. The kids didn't know that there are many men by the name of Kim, but to make it easier for him we started calling him by his first name, David. He was in 5th grade and Daran in 3rd grade at this time.

David and Daran decided to make some money during the warmer weather. In the Philippines, at many stoplights, there would be kids selling things or begging. They noticed nobody was doing this in the States! What a great opportunity for them to capture this clientele! They set up a lemonade stand near the stoplight a block from our house. When the cars would stop for the red light, they would go up to the cars and offer to sell them a refreshing drink. This was such a novel idea to the drivers that they bought just out of fun! The boys made quite a bit of money doing this. Such smart kids! I think this was the beginning of their entrepreneurial personalities being expressed.

Our older three children had all taken piano lessons in the Philippines. We had no piano in the USA, so we decided to buy an accordion and have Daran take lessons. There were actually accordion bands, so Daran got a chance to perform in them as well. It was a big thing for kids to do at that time; however, by the time of our next furlough four years later, we could not find an accordion anywhere.

During this furlough, Debi was home with me. We had lots of fun together. She had her own little pink suitcase with all her little toys in it, and would play for hours with her dolls in make-believe. Sesame Street was the latest TV show for kids, but our TV did not have this channel, so I prayed for a TV with VHS so she could watch Sesame Street. The very next day I got a call asking me if we could use a TV with VHS. Exactly what we needed! This hour of TV gave me the time I desired for meditation and prayer.

I was asked to speak at various women's groups, and would always share with them my testimony of how God met me in my lowest time in the Philippines. I was careful not to tell too much about it, because at that time my experience of being filled with the Holy Spirit was not practiced in the Baptist churches. However, women would come up to me afterward and share how they, too, had experienced this phenomenon. Soon it was known that I had had a Charismatic experience, and I was brought before the Mission's Board at the Annual Conference in June. The decision was that I had to give up my gift of tongues or we could not go back to the Philippines as their missionaries! We had one month to make this decision.

This was very heartbreaking for me. I didn't think it was fair to Fred to have his whole life changed because of me. I kept praying for God to show me what to do. Fred was ready to resign from the Mission, but I wasn't sure. Three days before we had to give our answer, we got a telephone call from Loren Cunningham, who started the YWAM mission. (His books are available.) I had never met the man, but he had prophesied over Fred at a conference about 18 months before that, although there would be a "death of the vision" in Fred's life, God would bring greater fruit from it.

I told Loren what was going on in our lives; he suggested I look at Ecclesiastes 11:1, *"Cast your bread upon the waters and after many days you will find it again."* I meditated on that and felt the Lord telling me to lay down my gift of tongues, believing He would let me "find it again" full and overflowing.

The very next day, Sunday, I woke up terribly sick. Fred rushed me to the hospital. An ultrasound revealed that I had a big mass in my abdomen. Prayer went up for me all over the USA. The suspicion was that I had cancer. My Bible Study group came to the hospital to visit and to pray for me. I was so surprised that they were all crying. I hadn't been told what the suspicion was!

Fortunately, surgery revealed no cancer. But endometriosis was found in the intestines, and I had five inches of my intestines removed People at the church brought cooked food to our household every day for the next two weeks while I recuperated. They were such a loving and caring church.

We did go back to the Philippines, but I was not allowed to use my gift of tongues, even in private worship. This was very difficult for me. Every time I would begin to pray I had the urge of the Holy Spirit to worship in tongues and I had to say "no." I felt like I was refusing God, and I would burst into tears. But after a few months Fred released me from this unprincipled demand. By the next June, the BGC had made the decision that each person had the right to worship God privately as they felt led.

I had to stay in the USA to recuperate from the operation so we sent Kevin on ahead to the Philippines when he was only 15 so he would not miss any more school. Fred left with the other school-age children a couple of weeks later; Debi and I stayed at a friend's house until I was able to travel.

Soon we were all back together again, but this time in Manila. We were sent there to be the first BGC missionaries commissioned to plant Baptist Churches in that city of 12 million people. What happened next was another great move of God in our lives!

Chapter 12
(1979-1981)

MANILA LIFE
"Blossom where you are planted."

We soon settled into a five-bedroom, one-story house in Antonio Village located in the suburb of Pasig. Four of the children were picked up by school bus each morning at about 6:30 am for a one-hour drive to attend Faith Academy. They would return by bus at around 3 pm, or on a later bus if they stayed for after school activities,

Kevin was now in 10th grade and was excelling not only academically, but also in wrestling and soccer. When he was a junior, he took first place in the wrestling tournament and was chosen to play in the tournaments with 16 other schools from the Far East in Japan, but we didn't have the money to send him. This is one of my great regrets; we thought we would save up money so he could go when he was a senior. However, he broke his leg wrestling as a senior and never got to go. The broken leg, however, was a blessing in disguise. Where his leg broke, they found pre-cancer cells that had caused the break. Since then, in his yearly tests they have never found these cells again. What an answer to prayer! At this time David was in 6th grade and Daran in 4th. Soon they would also excel in sports like their big brother.

Denise was now in 8th grade, and her expertise was in art. In fact, she was so good that in the 10th grade the teacher asked her to go down to the kindergarten and help teach art. Debi loved this because she was now in kindergarten. Denise also took lessons in piano and ballet. She had a quiet, caring disposition, and prides herself with the fact that she never got spanked! Even though she is 10 years older than Debi, they have become very close friends through the years.

We found a little pre-school just a block from our house for Debi. Of course, she was the little princess because she was the only American. All the other children spoke Tagalog, but she did make some friends and seemed to be happy there for a couple of hours each day. She would invite her new friends over for play sometimes in the afternoons. This was a very special time for me to have with Debi. I taught her to read at home using the Highlights magazine.

The next school year, we decided to see if Debi could be accepted at Faith Academy. Since Debi would not be five years old until November 27, she was too young to go to kindergarten except by special permission. When we had her tested, she was above her age level and they accepted her.

However, we realized there was another problem: the long day at school. She would have to leave at 6:30 am and not get home until 3 pm. We decided not to send her that year and just continued teaching her at home. By the next year, she was so advanced that they sent her up to first grade for reading. We had gotten her into a book club where she received a new book every month. These books were very helpful in motivating her to read, so she was already a good reader by the time she started school. She still remembers some of the books and has found copies of them so she can read them to her children.

While the children were getting settled again in school, I was looking around to see how God wanted me to reach out to others in our neighborhood. We decided to hold a Vacation Bible School at our house. The children came for Bible stories, songs, and crafts every day for two weeks. At the closing program the children shared with their parents what they had learned. These children had memorized about 10 verses each, along with learning many stories from the Bible. They also enjoyed the crafts they made each day. I do hope that the seeds of God's plan for their lives grew, and that many of them became ardent followers of Jesus. God promises that "His Word will not return unto Him void, but will accomplish the purpose for which it was sent." I take confidence in this promise that our work was not in vain.

I also started a Bible Study with about 10 ladies in the home of a neighbor, and it lasted for about four years. I believe they all came to know Jesus personally during that time, and really grew in following Jesus' teachings according to the Scriptures. I remember that some were reticent to join the class, so they asked their priest if it was all right; he gave his permission.

During Christmas vacation that first year, a group of carolers came to our door. We discovered they were a youth group from a nearby neighborhood. They invited us to attend their group. This is when we met the leaders, Joe and Cora Patag. They were schoolteachers, and saw how much the youth needed direction from God in their lives. Joe started this group that met weekly in his home. Joe invited us to come and start a church using the youth group as the base. It wasn't long before the Bag-ong Ilog Church was born. Soon the church was able to call and support a pastor.

One day, Fred got an invitation to visit a Saturday men's breakfast; the Bible Study was taught by another missionary. Eventually this other missionary teacher left for furlough, and the group asked Fred to be their teacher. These were mostly wealthy Catholic business men in the area who had experienced the Baptism of the Holy Spirit and were hungry to study the Bible. They liked Fred's method of teaching because he let them discover truth for themselves. Soon they also asked Fred to start an evening class for them and their wives. Next they wanted a group for their youth. It was one of these nights, when the youth were leaving our house, that the story in Chapter I about Fred being held at gunpoint took place.

Soon the men came to Fred and said, "We've been reading in the Bible how the new believers were baptized, so we want to be baptized too; will you baptize us?" These men had never seen a baptism of adults by immersion. So Fred asked them to plan the event.

They decided to rent a bus for all of them to go together to the beach house of Narciso Padilla, one of the members. On the bus they had a loud speaker so all the men could give their testimonies, interspersed with singing worship songs. Rudy Topacio led them with his guitar. At the beach, they all went into the water up to their waist. Fred baptized them. As each one came up out of the water praise and worship would break out. It took about 2 hours to baptize these 11 men! One of the men, Henry Canoy, had had a stroke and was slightly paralyzed, so they had to take him out to the deeper water on a raft so he could confirm his commitment to follow Jesus.

When their wives heard about this, they too wanted to be baptized along with some of the youth. Our whole family got to go on that trip. What joy and excitement these new believers experienced!

We didn't start a church with these people. They each found their own places of worship, and all became active in sharing Christ with others in various ways. Some of them started their own churches.

Because Fred had found Mass Media to be such an effective tool for Evangelism in Cebu, he wanted to get involved with this in Manila. Narciso Padilla, a multi-millionaire who attended Fred's Bible Studies, asked Fred to come and help him start a Christian TV station. Unfortunately, the station never got on the air because the Marcos government would not give them a permit. Some say it was because they refused to pay a bribe. The prophecy given years before by Loren Cunningham came true. Fred never got back into Media again except for two occasions: to teach Bible Studies to the staff of a local radio station, and to serve as a "judge" on Ronald Remy's (another multimillionaire, former vice-governor Quezon City, and movie star who attended Fred's Bible Study) popular program on TV that had nation-wide coverage.

God had other plans for us as well. One day while I was teaching a Bible Study on Jesus and Peter walking on the water, I realized God was speaking to me, saying, "Ruth, if you, like Peter, take my hand, get out of the boat, and you, too, will walk on water with me. But you must keep your eyes on me. Then I will abundantly supply all your needs." I began to weep and wondered what God was really saying to me.

In the meantime, God had been speaking to Fred from the story of Abraham's calling from God to leave his land and go to a place He would show him. That night, when we shared these experiences with each other, we realized God was leading us to leave the BGC Mission in order to work cross-denominationally with Catholics!

This was a very big decision; we had five children to support, school tuition, rent, and all the other living expenses. Could God REALLY be telling us to just resign from the Mission and trust Him alone to supply all our needs?

Fred decided to get confirmation about this decision, so he wrote letters to 20 people he highly respected about how God had spoken to us. 19 responses were positive, encouraging us to follow what God was saying to us.

At the Philippine Annual Conference in April of 1980, we handed in our resignation. Some seemed sorry to see us go, but they confirmed that our decision was the right one. We were given six months' severance pay and the use of the vehicle we were driving. Taking Denise with him, Fred decided to go back to the States to visit some of the churches that invited us. After three of these churches heard our story and our vision for the future, they decided to help support us.

It was amazing to me where all our support came from. Let me tell some of the more spectacular ways God took care of us.

The Filipino groups we were teaching suddenly decided to take offerings at our Bible Studies for us. They knew nothing about our leaving the mission. This was definitely the Holy Spirit putting this on their hearts.

When I arrived to teach one Bible Study, the women wanted me to teach them about tithing, so I quickly changed my talk and tried the best I could to show them Scriptures about the principles of tithing. After I left that day, they got out the tables to play their favorite game, Mahjong. Of course a little gambling went along with it. Later in the afternoon I heard someone calling from the gate, "*Tao po*" – "hello." There at my gate was the maid of the lady where we held our Bible Study. She handed me an envelope and left. I was shocked when I opened the envelope and found about one hundred pesos! (About $30 at that time.) The note read: "Thank you for teaching us today about tithing; we decided to tithe our earnings from Mahjong today." I burst into laughter! I thought, "Next time I better teach them about gambling." After that they decided to take an offering for me at every Bible Study. The Bible Study was the day before I sent my cook to market, and it was often just what we needed to buy fresh food for the coming week.

Another day, I again heard someone at the gate calling (the Filipino way of knocking or ringing a doorbell). This time it was an American. With a great big smile he said, "Do you remember me?" Strangely, I recognized the smile, but not the face. His name was Stanley Erickson.

He reminded me that 25 years before he was a classmate of Fred's at Bethel College. He said he was now a businessman in Singapore. When he needed to make a trip to Manila, just an hour's flight away, he suddenly remembered that we were in Manila and decided to try to find us. What a joy it was to have him spend a few days with us!

He specifically asked how our ministry was going. We got to share with him the great things God was doing. A few weeks later, we received in the mail a $50 check, which he continued to send every month for the next few years. He also told his church in Singapore about our ministry, and one family decided also to send us $50 a month.

God truly did supply all our needs, and we did our part by carefully budgeting. I tried to stretch a pound of hamburger by mixing it with "veggie meal," but eventually the boys discovered what I was doing and that was the end of that.

Another trick I tried was buying jeans one size larger, hemming them up and letting out the hems as the boys grew. The problem was that the hemline had turned white so I used a blue indelible pen and colored in the white line.

Another blessing was that the money exchange rate changed in our favor. We were paying our rent in dollars to owners who lived in the States, so we realized we could save a lot of money by paying in pesos for a house with cheaper rent. After a few months, we found a house in Green Hills in a gated, 200-home community. It had one less bedroom, but we decided to partition off half of Fred's office for sleeping quarters for Debi, who was now in 4th grade. This would be David's last year before college, and Denise and Kevin were already in the USA attending college.

This was an ideal place because the children could ride their bikes to the little mall just yards away from the front gate. Furthermore, we were in a gated community with high walls around it; no one could enter without proper identification.

We did have a scary experience in our move to the new house. Fred had mixed a poisonous black-looking solution to paint on the posts of the house to keep off the wood-eating termites. He kept this *under* the sink in the kitchen (no name on the jar). I also had a black-looking coffee concentrate that I kept in a jar *in* the refrigerator also unmarked. In the move these two jars got mixed up. The poison one got put in the refrigerator.

In the morning, I got Fred a cup of coffee made with this poison. He took one sip and realized what it was. Poison! Fred immediately called his doctor who told him to come to the prayer breakfast that day so they could pray for him! That's exactly what they did, and Fred never had any stomach problems or adverse effects from the poison. God is so good!

We always had many pets. One day, I was getting a little exercise by riding my bike around the streets inside the gated community and took our big dog with me. Suddenly, he jumped in front of the bike and I went flying. There were no cell phones in those days, so I lay on the hard cement yelling for help. I was in a great deal of pain and just couldn't get up. I know the dog felt bad because he kept coming over and licking my face.

Soon one of the maids of a neighbor came by and saw me. I asked her to please go to my house and get help. Soon Fred came with the car and took me to emergency. They had to put a steel pin in the shoulder. My arm works fine today, but I still have a bone sticking up.

After we left the Mission, we felt it necessary to find a "spiritual covering" -- a group through which we could receive nurturing and channel funds. Dr. Harold Sala of Guidelines for Family Living came to the Philippines about once or twice a year to hold Marriage

Enrichment Seminars. Through the intervention of our friends, Dick and Helen Cadd, we decided to ask if he would accept us, which he did. For two years we were under this covering.

Fred and I had also started holding Marriage Enrichment classes on our own. We used the Southern Baptist material called "Philosophy of Christian Womanhood" as a basis. This was set up as a 10-week study. We adapted the material so we could use it with couples. Fred taught the men and I taught the women. Debi would often come and be our registrar. Our "modus operandi" was to charge for this course. We held them at a private club, thus reaching a more affluent class of people. Every Saturday for 11 weeks, we met from 10:00 a.m. until 3:00 p.m., including a lunch break. This attracted many hurting people.

It was always such a blessing to hear the testimonies of how much these classes had meant to the people. I'll never forget one lady who said, "What I learned most from this class is that Jesus Christ loves me and died for me and I have decided to follow Him." I believe we held these classes twice a year for about five years; our attendance was between 20 and 30 people. Years later I ran into a lady who told me how she was still applying the lessons she learned in our classes, and that her marriage was going great.

This was a great time to be in ministry in Manila. The Holy Spirit was moving in powerful ways — one was through all-night prayer meetings often attended by the youth. At one of these prayer meetings, Fred met Steve Mirpuri and soon was meeting with him regularly to help him to grow in his new life in Christ. His conversion story is quite amazing, so I thought it worthwhile to tell here.

Steve was a drug addict on the streets. One day, a little old man gave him a little booklet about Jesus and how he could become His follower. Because of this, Steve turned his life around and started coming to the all-night prayer meetings. He had held many jobs in the past, but would always get fired because of his addiction to drugs. But now he was a new creature in Christ —"old things had passed away and all things had become new." He decided to try to get a job again in sales. At his interview, he told the interviewer the whole story of his messed up life, and then he said, "Sir, I know there is no reason why you should hire me, but if you will give me a chance, I will become your best salesman." Mr. Linda Tampons, the boss, went home that night and couldn't get Steve's testimony out of his mind; he had never heard anything like that before. He thought, "There is no good reason I should hire this guy." But try as he may, he couldn't get him out of his mind. (We believe the Holy Spirit wouldn't let him.) The next day Steve got the job! As promised, Steve became the best salesman. As his boss watched Steve's life continue to change he, too, became a follower of Jesus, and Fred disciple him as well.

In time, Steve felt God calling him to study for the ministry, and four years later he graduated from seminary at the top of his class. We then met the little old man — now very wrinkled and walking with a cane -- who had led Steve to the Lord. What a joy for us! Steve married Rose, and after pastoring a large church in the Manila area, decided to begin a ministry reaching out to the poor. We were privileged to see them when we visited in 2001. Fred saw them more recently in 2011.

Another sphere of ministry during this time was "Ang Ligaya ng Panginoon" (Joy of the Lord Community). Mac and Rhoda Bradshaw had teamed up with a German Jesuit Priest, Fr. Herb Schneider, to start an ecumenical community in 1976. In 1980, this community numbered over 2,000.

The way to join the community was to go through the "Life in the Spirit" seminar, which gave the basics to becoming a follower of Jesus. This was followed by a weekend retreat leading to the Baptism of the Holy Spirit (which is actually a true conversion experience).

We decided this would be a great way to join God in what He was doing in the Roman Catholic Church. We developed great friendships with these wonderful, Spirit-filled Catholics, and even became pastoral leaders of 10 people. We met weekly in our home for Bible Study, worship, and prayer, and every Sunday afternoon with all 2,000. We formed a very strong bond with these dear friends. Even 19 years after leaving the Philippines, when we go back to visit, Bob and Betsy Tenchavez, who use to be in our group, hold welcome-back parties for us with many of our former friends in Ligaya. What a joy to see them and to hear their stories of how God has been blessing them, as they generously help the poor and serve Him in other ways as the Spirit leads them.

We always had household help (maids) in the Philippines. These were usually young girls who came right from the farm. Some had never seen a flush toilet before. It was my joy to teach them how to cook, clean, and do laundry with a wringer-type machine. They were always so joyful and dearly loved our children. But sometimes having household help brought challenges as well. One girl I hired in Manila turned out to be a thief and stole jewelry and money. One day, I found my purse emptied out in the yard, but when I went to find the girl, she had disappeared and we never saw her again.

But we also saw many of the girls come to faith in Jesus. Esther, who worked for us for seven years when the children were small, got a job as a cook, at the private company club of Atlas Fertilizer, when we left Toledo City. Today she has her own little bakery in a small town on the northern coast of Cebu. Another girl, Indi, came from an orphanage; she worked for us while going to secretarial school. Today she is the secretary for the CEO of the SIL Mission (Wycliffe) in Manila. Having household help allowed me time to be involved in teaching Bible Studies and discipling women.

Speaking of Bible Studies -- Helen Cadd and I teamed up and taught a Bible Study in the home of Billie Padilla, a Cuban, every Saturday morning for two years. Billie had met her husband, Narciso (Ciso) Padilla, while she was studying in Boston and he was getting his masters at MIT. After they married in Cuba, Castro pressured the wealthy to leave the country. They were only allowed one suitcase each when they left. The government took over their beautiful home for their own purposes.

In 1976, during the Billy Graham Crusade in Manila, Billie and Ciso decided to follow Jesus. Billie had asked Helen and me to come each Saturday and teach her Spanish-speaking friends the Bible. We would teach and Billie would interpret. Many of them decided to follow Jesus, and Fred had the privilege of baptizing some of them. I loved teaching this class with Helen, but it did take me away from my own family every Saturday morning; that was such a great sacrifice!

One Saturday when I came home, our five-year-old Debi came running to me and said, "Know what I did today, Mommy? I was watching a man speak on TV and he said to put my hand on the TV and he would pray for me to ask Jesus into my heart." She had a great big smile on her face, and her eyes were beaming.

It was such a joy to watch Debi grow in her love for and faith in Jesus. Later when we moved to Green Hills, she would often go across the street to the Catholic Church and pray. She would also write letters to God. I could see that at a very young age, she already knew what it meant to love and to follow Jesus.

In 1981, just before Christmas, we decided that we needed a short furlough to the States. We missed our eldest son, Kevin, who had left for college three months before. It was such a joy to see him again and to know he was doing well.

We flew straight to Michigan where my sister-in-law, Carol, met us with winter coats for everyone. She and her husband, Jerry, hosted us for the weekend. After visiting with my family we drove to Wisconsin to see Fred's family. Then we headed for DeKalb, IL, where Fred was scheduled to speak on Sunday morning. The children were farmed out to different homes, as no one family could house all of us. Denise and Debi were together, and David and Daran at another home. However, the weather turned extremely cold -- 65 degrees below zero wind-chill, and much ice and snow. The church decided not to have a service that day, so Fred never got to preach. We left the next morning for warmer weather. When we got to New Mexico and pulled into a motel, Fred got out of the car; not realizing the ground was icy, he had a bad fall and broke his right wrist. We had to go to emergency and have a cast put on. After that I got to write all the checks!

It was during this time that we began attending the Vineyard Christian Fellowship in Long Beach. We needed to find a new covering for our mission, and they were willing to do that for us. They also paid our health care insurance for the family for the next five years. All our finances were channeled through them. Having this wonderful church connection was such a blessing for us. It was like truly "coming home." We had found a home where our beliefs and passions really fit in.

We lived in Fountain Valley for those six months in a condominium. Kevin also came to live with us during that time. It was so good to have him home again.

Debi went to second grade there. The first day of class, the teacher, trying to honor her, asked her to lead the class in the National Anthem. What an embarrassment for Debi! She only knew the Philippine National Anthem.

David and Denise had to cross the freeway on an overpass to get to the high school. The police stopped them as Denise was riding on the back of David's bike; being foreigners, they didn't know this was against the law. Fred had to go with David to bicycle court.

Denise had a chance to babysit often that summer for two darling little preschoolers whose mother was an actress and seldom home. She also met a friend with whom she stayed the following summer before she left for Azusa Pacific College.

This six-month break helped us so much to refocus and find a church home. But we had a big problem: we needed $5,000 for airfares and to buy a used car for Kevin. But we'll save this great story for the next chapter.

Chapter 13
(1982-1985)

GOD'S AMAZING PROVISIONS
"And see if I will not pour out blessings from heaven..."

Since we didn't have the money for airfare, we began to wonder if God wanted us to go back to the Philippines. But the Lord spoke to Fred during one of the church services at the Vineyard from Isaiah: *"The islands are calling to you; they're calling to you with hope."* Feeling that God was telling us to go back, he ordered our tickets from the Dutch company, Siama, which gave discounted airline tickets to missionaries. They would be sent C.O.D., so we had to have the money by the time the tickets arrived.

Kevin also needed a car. We found one for $2,500 that was in good condition so we put $500 down on it, also trusting God to provide the rest of the money. All totaled, we needed $5,000 by July 1st. We told no one about this need, but we prayed fervently. By June 30th, still no money had come.

At 6 pm that evening the phone rang. I was surprised when I answered that it was Dr. Harold Sala, with whom we had worked for the previous two years doing follow-up from his marriage counseling seminars in Manila. He asked, "Have you been asking God for a certain amount of money?" "Yes!" I responded. He said, "How much?" I said, "$5,000." "You got it!" he shouted. Then he explained how it happened.

He was having lunch with a wealthy businessman in hopes of getting money for his own ministry; instead the man asked, "By the way how are the Thomas's doing?" Harold answered, "Well, I think they are doing fine and will soon be returning to the Philippines. Then the man wrote out a check for us for $5,000, and said, "I just feel God wants me to give this to them." We had never met the man, but he had heard about our ministry. (A year later when we were back in Manila, Dr. Sala visited us and gave us another $5,000 from this same man. Denise was about to leave for college, so this was God's provision for me to take her to the States and get her settled at Azusa Pacific University.)

Soon we said a sad goodbye to Kevin, but we were happy we had been able to buy him a car.

Back in Manila, 1982 was filled with great ministry opportunities. We continued teaching our Bible Studies and our 11-week Marriage Enrichment Seminars. Because of these involvements, we got invited to minister to some of the affluent classes of people in Manila. They may be wealthy, but with wealth often comes a great deal more problems. One of the biggest problems involved men having "*caritas*" (kept women, not their wives). In fact, it is a sign of wealth for men to afford this "luxury." We often got called on to minister to these broken people. One time we were asked to minister to about 12 couples who had experienced God's forgiving love and were desirous to now have God heal their marriages. This weekend retreat, held at President Cory Aquino's farm, saw God bring repentance, forgiveness, and healing to these couples.

The Ligaya ng Panginoon Community (Joy of the Lord Community) decided to start a businessmen's breakfast to reach these "wayward" men. At their breakfasts, they would sing some songs and then listen to the testimony of one of the men whose life had been transformed by God. After a few months of these breakfasts, the Life in the Spirit seminar was offered to these men, with the provision that they had to bring their wives if they wanted to attend.

Fred and I were table leaders for a group of five couples during this "Life in the Spirit" seminar. Our goal was to meet with them weekly and to see how they were responding to the teachings. The overall goal was to bring each couple to a place of commitment to

Jesus. Then these couples would be invited to attend a weekend retreat where the Baptism of the Holy Spirit would be emphasized.

After a few weeks, all but one couple in our group had committed their lives to Christ. The husband of this last couple was a powerful man in the government. His job was to oversee all the sugar plantation owners. When these men came to Manila for their meetings, he was to entertain them. Part of that entertainment was to supply them with phone numbers of women. He also was quite a skeptic; Fred challenged him to read the New Testament before he met with him. Fred and I prayed fervently for this last couple. Our hearts were heavy as we headed for the restaurant to meet with them. The wife and I sat at a separate table than the husband and Fred. As I talked with the wife she responded easily to committing her life to the Lord. But I was wondering how the husband was responding as Fred talked with him.

Later I learned that before Fred could say much of anything to him, the husband told Fred, "I have read through the New Testament and I have had all my questions answered; I am ready now to commit my life to Jesus." Later this man stood up in front of all the sugar plantation owners and gave his testimony of committing his life to Jesus. Then, as he tore up the little black book with all the call girls' phone numbers in it, he said, "And from now on I will no longer be doing this."

Another couple, Jun and Josie Torno, also came to Christ about this time. They, too, had a rocky marriage. We were privileged to see them in 2009 again after 25 years, still faithful to the Lord. Josie has cancer, but has used this as a platform to tell of God's great love and salvation. I was surprised when, about two years ago, I received an email from her with an attached video of her sharing her testimony during an interview on a TV talk show.

After one year back in Manila, Denise graduated from Faith Academy. I took her back to the States and got her settled at Azusa Pacific University. She stayed there just one year, and then transferred to Long Beach State while Kevin was attending Long Beach City College. They got an apartment together with one other person. A year later I went back to visit them for a few weeks. Kevin eventually went on to graduate from Cal State Los Angeles.

Since we didn't have the ability to finance our children's college education, they all had to work. They worked very hard to support themselves so they could pay their tuitions and living expenses. Most of them finished college with no debts!

David had just two more years left at Faith Academy. He enjoyed wrestling, and I remember him being so much taller than his opponents. He did well, but he really excelled in soccer and became the captain of the team in his senior year. He was also voted class president that year.

Daran, following in the footsteps of his two brothers, was also an outstanding athlete, except that he chose to play basketball and volleyball. He excelled in both of these sports, and went to the Far East tournament in his senior year as co-captain of the Volleyball team. I think they took 4th place out of 16 schools.

Debi was continuing to grow into a very good artist and writer. She also took piano lessons, but had been asking for a flute since she was in 1st grade. Now, in 3rd grade, she was still praying for a flute. We decided to include her request in our monthly prayer letters to our supporters in the States. Amazing things happened.

One of the members in Fred's home church in Racine, Wisconsin got our prayer letter. They took it with them on a trip to see family in Connecticut. Her daughter-in-law's father had a junk yard where cars that had been totaled in accidents were stored. People would come to buy parts off these cars; this was his business. They gave the letter to her parents to read. When the father saw the request of Debi for a flute, he remembered, "I think I saw an instrument in the back seat of one of cars just brought in," he said. He went out to get it. Sure enough it was a flute -- and not only that, but the very best kind of flute for a beginner -- the Gemeinhardt brand. They soon had the flute in the mail. What joy for Debi when she saw again how God answered her prayers!

It was great watching Debi's character develop. She wasn't afraid to stand up for what was right. When a Catholic girl in her class was being ridiculed, Debi stood up for her. When a Korean girl who knew no English joined her class, Debi was right alongside her helping her learn English.

When David finished high school, we decided to all go back to the States for a year's furlough. Fred's uncle had died and left him $5,000 from an insurance policy, so Fred took David on a tour through Europe on the way back to the States. David was very interested in architecture at that time, and we thought this trip would expose him to various architectural structures in various countries. He eventually became a Civil Engineer instead.

Daran, Debi, and I stopped off in Korea for one night and spent the whole time there shopping for athletic shoes for all the kids, as well as leather items and sweaters. I remember getting Denise a pink Angora sweater. It's amazing the things one remembers, and also the things one forgets.

We were praying much about where we were going to live for a year while in the States. One day while I was shopping in Manila, I saw another missionary whom I didn't know very well, but as we talked I told her about our need for a house in the USA. Through her connections, we were able to get a four-bedroom house in Long Beach for $600 a month. Her parents who owned the house were coming to the Philippines to teach in their mission's school for one year. This worked out perfectly. God again took care of our need! "Where He guides, He provides!" became our motto.

The year in the States was a lot of fun. Denise and Kevin came home to live with us. David was now a freshman at Long Beach State where Kevin and Denise were studying.

Soon David and Denise joined the Long Beach State rowing team. Denise was a coxswain for one of the boats. They would get up early each morning and be out on the water by 5 am. We enjoyed watching them compete with other schools. Often David would bring home his whole rowing team for breakfast. We had fun making pancakes for these eight guys.

Fred insisted that we buy a microwave -- the latest new invention on the market. I wasn't too excited about it, but Daran was; he went with me to all the cooking classes to learn how to use it. Today he is a fabulous Gourmet cook. But no microwaves for him! He cooks everything from scratch.

Daran's high school was about four miles away, so we bought him a small scooter -- I think they called it a "doodle-bug" -- so he could have more independence. He did very well that year in school. I'll never forget the day he came home and showed me all A's on his report card. What a blessing that was for us because, as a 1st grader, he had trouble learning to read. He wore glasses for a few years, but I think it may have been dyslexia, which no one knew about in those days. I found out later that this runs on my side of the family.

Daran excelled tremendously in basketball that year, but was "black-listed" by the coach for choosing to go on a Thanksgiving Holiday ski trip with his family instead of playing basketball. We were so glad he chose to go with us. I think he had his priorities right!

That was a very special vacation. My cousin, Jane, and her husband, Dave, offered their vacation home for the long weekend in the White Mountains of Arizona. They even supplied us with some of the skiing equipment. None of us had ever been skiing before, but by the end of the day David and Daran had conquered the heights of every ski lift from the easiest to the hardest. Fred also was doing "quite" well on the short ski runs. I stayed with Debi on the "bunny" hill, but finally decided to try the shortest ski lift. Fred and I went up together on the lift; I fell three times coming down, but at least I did it -- my one and only time to ever ski. I can see why people love it so much.

Debi's school was just across the street from the house. She seemed to enjoy fifth grade there and she could come home for lunch. She excelled so much that they decided to give her a gifted-child test. She cried when she got one point below the genius level. She thought she had failed! Apparently the teacher didn't explain what this meant.

Debi, however, wanted so much to have a dog. I told her she could have a dog, but it would have to be free, as we didn't have the money to buy one. The next Sunday in church, she wrote out a prayer request and showed it to me. It said, "Dear God, please may I have a dog by tomorrow morning by 10:00 a.m.? Love, Debi." After showing me the note, she put her prayer request in the offering plate as it came around. I was quietly praying too, "Oh God, how do we help you answer her prayer request?" I shouldn't have been worried. As we were leaving the church service, there was a picture of an adorable blonde cocker spaniel on the bulletin board with a note: "Free for anyone who can give this dog a good home." This dog was soon ours.

Peachy, the Cocker Spaniel that Debi had prayed for, was a wonderful pet. She was very loveable and could even do tricks. There was a stray cat in the neighborhood that made friends with Peachy and would also bring little "gifts," like dead birds, to our doorstep. She was trying to wedge her way into our family. Finally, we took her in. She and Peachy played together every day. But one day, the cat gave birth to six kittens in the garage. Peachy tried to help her move the kittens into the house by carrying them in her mouth just like the cat did, without realizing how strong her bite was. She killed every one that she carried. How sad!

We soon realized that our finances were not enough to support this growing family. I had a degree in teaching, but I had never gotten my credential for teaching. However, if I passed the CBEST test I could do substitute teaching. I was told there was a lot of geometry on the test. I had never studied geometry, so I asked my sons to teach me. They must have done a good job because I learned enough to pass the test, and was approved to substitute in the elementary schools. But we needed another miracle. If I did get a teaching job, I had no transportation! The day before I got my first call to substitute, Owen Schumacher came up to me in church and asked if we could use another vehicle at our house. He had a pick-up truck just sitting in his yard that he would be glad to loan us. He brought it over that afternoon. When the call came the next morning, I was ready! Soon I was substituting about three days a week. When I got my first paycheck, the first thing I did (after tithing) was to buy Denise a sewing machine and a carpet for her bedroom.

Fred drove to Riverside every day to work for his brother, Chuck, in his business, Benchmark Clock Company. So God provided by giving us jobs. We continued to attend the Vineyard Christian Fellowship church in Long Beach, but wondered if God wanted us to stay in the States or return to the Philippines. At this point, we no longer had the financial base we needed to return.

Then one day, a letter came from the Union Church of Manila offering Fred to come on staff as a part-time associate pastor. We now knew what we were supposed to do. Soon we were packing up again to go back to our home in Green Hills. But this time only Daran and Debi would be going with us.

Chapter 14
(1986-1991)

UNION CHURCH
"Our times are in His Hands"

It was good that we could settle back into our house in Greenhills; we had sub-leased it for a year while we were on furlough. With David now in the USA in his second year of college, Debi got to have her own room.

The first thing she asked to do was to paint it. The walls were white with navy blue trim, so we let her do whatever she wanted. When we came home one day, she had a surprise for us: there were handprints and footprints in multi-colors very artistically painted all over her walls! We loved watching her gifts blossom!

Daran was now a senior in high school. He continued to excel in his grades and in volleyball and basketball. He needed a very heavy breakfast to build up his body for sports, so every morning I was up early cooking rice and beef tapa. He had a very winsome personality too, always seeing the funny side of most anything. But at the same time, he had deep feelings and thoughts. In later years he took a writing course at Duke University, and learned more about how to express these feelings on paper. The professor really encouraged him to do more of this. I understand he has started writing a book, but has it "on hold" at present.

At the end of the school year, we let him have a party at our house with a DJ. I heard they had a great time! (We had left the house.) He made Debi stay in her room, however, during the party. We should have taken her with us. We made a lot of mistakes in parenting our children. It's amazing to us how well they turned out in spite of this.

After graduation, we took Daran to Hong Kong for a few days; we bought him a stereo and celebrated his 18th birthday there. Then he flew back to the USA to live with Kevin and get a job before starting college in the fall. It was so hard to see him leave -- we all missed him tremendously, especially Debi.

We had hoped Daran would try for an athletic scholarship like his friend, Dan Landry. Dan got a full scholarship to UCLA in Volleyball, but Daran thought he was too short, only 6'1" and the "wrong color", especially for basketball. So he worked very hard at various jobs. I remember specifically when he worked at Circuit City, the manager offered to train him to be a manager, but he would have had to quit school. We were thankful that he asked Fred for advice. Fred encouraged him to stay in school, as there would be many more opportunities; this was just the "tip of the iceberg." He had many talents and abilities, and the world would discover him soon enough. We were right. He has excelled at every job he has ever had. Today, he has his own business in servicing and repairing high-end and foreign cars in Raleigh, NC.

After Daran left, Debi asked if we could home-school her for the 7th grade. She told me later that she wanted to get closer to her parents. This was a lot of fun, but after just one semester, she was ready to go back to school and get involved in school events again. We also got her a beautiful Persian cat and an adorable dog, but she still longed for her siblings, especially her sister.

That Christmas, our dear friend, Marlyn, paid the airfare for all of our children to come home to the Philippines for the holidays. What a blessing that was!

In the States, David had been invited to share a house with Owen, the man who loaned us his truck so I could drive to work. So, when Owen left to get married, all four of the children in college moved into this house. This way they could pool their resources. They even brought in another student to live there, which helped with the rent.

After one year, the Union Church decided to bring Fred on Staff full time and give him full benefits. This included one month of vacation each year. This was so wonderful! At least we got to see our four children in college each year!

That summer my mother, who was living in San Francisco near my sister, Karen, came down to Long Beach for a visit when we came home for a month. All of us, including Debi, stayed at this house the children had rented.

One day, I decided we would all walk to a park a few blocks away to have a picnic lunch. Before we left I put a load of clothes in the washing machine. About 2 hours later, we came home to find water running out of the front door! Apparently the hose on the washing machine broke and the water ran all over the house. Debi was the only one who thought of calling the fire department. We were all surprised when they arrived and cleaned up the water. However, the carpets were soaked. I remember us moving all the furniture out into the backyard and trying to lift the carpet up so it would dry. To keep the mood in the "party spirit," we all decided to take a dip in the pool. I really don't remember what happened next. It's one of those memories where I tend to only remember the fun parts!

Debi was now in eighth grade, and began praying that her sister, Denise, would come back to the Philippines. I think I mentioned early on that Debi was quite a pray-er. God answered so many amazing prayers for her. In fact, we in the family use to say, "If you want your prayers answered, just ask Debi to pray." The prayer for her sister to come back to the Philippines just seemed way too impossible. But we know that "nothing is impossible with God." Even with all her school and church involvements, she still kept praying for her sister to come back home. A year later this prayer would be answered.

In the meantime, Denise was getting close to graduating from college with a degree in Home Economics. Being her senior year, she had to do her practice teaching. One day we got a phone call from her from the States; she was crying on the phone that she wanted to come home. She really didn't like teaching after all. We told her to sell the car we had given her to buy her ticket.

We decided not to tell Debi that Denise was coming. The day she arrived, Debi was still in school, so we put Denise in Debi's bedroom. When Debi came home we told her we had a surprise for her. We blindfolded her and took her into her room and had her sit down on her bed. She immediately could feel something else was on the bed. She thought it was a dog. What joy when she took off her blindfold and found out it was Denise!

We had always felt that Denise should pursue a degree in some phase of art, so I called the prestigious Philippine School of Interior Design to see what the possibilities were of her studying there. They had just started classes that week, and she was allowed to enter.

Denise settled into her classes in graphic design for the next two years. She finished all her course work, but wasn't able to do her final project because we left for the States before it was due. One year later she got a job in Interior Design, and has since worked for three different companies in that field. She also re-designed three rooms in their church in Cottonwood, MN to include a café, a mission's corner, an artist corner and a lounge. In addition she helped put in a prayer garden facing the lake where people can come and meditate.

It was such a delight to have both the girls there. Even though they are 10 years apart in age, they have always been close. During those years, Denise got connected through her classmates with the elite Spanish crowd and made many close friends.

The girls decided they wanted to teach Sunday school at Union Church where Fred was pastoring, so Debi took the 2-year-olds and Denise the 4-year-olds. Denise wanted 4-year-olds because they very innocently would "tell her about what was going on in their families," sometimes very personal information! Apparently Denise enjoyed that!

In the meantime, Debi was excelling in writing, whether prose, poetry, or stories. I remember her starting a novel about "little people" who lived in the walls of a mansion. I was her greatest fan, and couldn't wait until she finished each next chapter so I could read it. Unfortunately, she only finished four chapters. I wish we could find the manuscripts.

Debi also enjoyed theater. She and a friend competed with a scene from Romeo and Juliet, which won first place. She also played the part of one of the nuns in a school production of "Sound of Music."

113

She likewise planned the most elaborate birthday parties. One such overnight party included an imaginary trip to Hawaii. She printed out boarding passes, menus for the airplane, and entertainment for the evening program. Her friends had to "pack" suitcases that would be received at the check-in counter before boarding the plane. The air-conditioned office (Fred's) was the plane. Menus she had made were passed out and our maids served them their dinner on trays. They watched a movie before going to sleep. The next morning they again got menus, and food was again delivered on trays. Soon the plane landed in Hawaii and they got their luggage and changed into Hawaiian dress. She also did another birthday party similar to this.

We really enjoyed ministering to the diverse congregation at Union Church. About 60% of the congregation was made up of foreigners from about 25 different countries. This was also a melting pot for those of various Christian persuasions. We loved the diversity. When my dad heard about this church, he commented on how amazing it was that all these diverse people could get along so well together, especially theologically. That had not been his experience in his church!

Fred became the administrative pastor, overseeing the daily workings of the church staff of about 20 people. Darrell Johnson, our senior pastor, was an excellent speaker, so the church grew to about 1,000 people in the congregation.

Another one of Fred's responsibilities was setting up small groups in the church. He also did personal counseling, weddings, and funerals. One day, a lady called him with a problem; it seemed she and her husband were arguing about whether they should tithe their gross or net income. They were Australians who had a stuffed toy business. They liked Fred, and soon were avid worshippers at Union. They were one of six couples who joined our weekly home group.

The Christian Education director asked if I would take over the Adult Education program for the church. I was delighted to do this. I developed a three-prong program, in which students could sign up to take one of the three classes each quarter. I would pull in excellent teachers and professors from the various missionary and Bible

College communities. We had two services on Sundays and offered three classes each hour. We also did a video series on various subjects with discussion groups.

Another aspect of my ministry at Union Church was being the Spiritual Director for the Women's Ministry. This entailed giving a devotional at each monthly meeting, or asking someone else to do it. The big event each year was the Women's Retreat. It was fun leading a team of about 10 women -- like running a business. At one of the retreats, I had a sister (nun) from the "Evangelical Sisterhood of Mary" come and speak. This ministry started in Germany during WW11. The speaker had us dancing during our worship time – quite unheard of at Union Church! Unbeknown to me there, was a reporter there and the next morning a picture was on the front page of the Manila Times with the caption under it, "I Danced with a Nun." This made quite a stir in the community! Nuns don't dance! I had to answer a lot of questions over this.

In 1990, Fred and I went back to the States for a break. We visited Kevin and Daran in their apartment in L.A. Daran's room was very neat and clean, but Kevin's was, let's say, in need of some adjustments. Daran even made a video of the differences (with a few very funny additions). It is hilarious!

We also visited a Christian community in Minneapolis that was a sister group to Ligaya in the Philippines, called "The Body of Christ." Fred had been in contact with Larry Alberts, the leader of this community since 1985. At that time, Larry had expressed an interest in Fred coming and working with him at some point in the future.

We were so impressed with these people; most of them lived within walking distance of each other. Many home-schooled their children, but most impressive of all was how they shared their lives on a daily basis. The men met each morning at 6 am for prayer before they headed off to work. The women met each Saturday morning for prayer. Each Sunday evening these people, who were both Catholics and Protestants, met for worship and fun times together. They also helped one another with daily tasks and supported one another through difficult times. I felt like I had found what I had been longing for -- a real extended family!

During our prayer time with them, they discerned that we should come and be part of their community. Afterwards, we walked over to the Lilly's house for dinner. I saw an English Tudor-style house next door to theirs and was drawn to it. I actually took a picture of it as I thought, "The girls would love living in a house like this." When I asked the Lilly's if it was for sale, they said, "Well, not yet, but the people are planning to sell it in a year and retire." Was God trying to tell us something? As it turned out, a year later we bought this house and moved to this community.

Back in Manila, we continued our ministries in Ligaya ng Panginoon Community (Joy of the Lord) as well as at Union Church. Rev. Darrel Johnson, who had now been pastor at UCM for four years, felt called to leave and take a pastorate in Sacramento. Gordon Smith became the new pastor. These were difficult times for Fred; everything seemed to change at the church.

We decided to go on a four-day prayer and fasting retreat at the country home of our friends, Jim and Linda Murray, to decide whether we should stay at UCM or accept the offer at the Body of Christ in Minneapolis. At the end of the four days, we felt God had shown us through Scripture and prayer that we were to return to the USA at the end of the school year. We also sought advice from people we respected, like Fr. Herb Schneider, the leader of Ligaya. Fr. Herb said that these were the most important years of our children's lives, and that they needed us more now than ever as they were making lasting decisions for their futures. This seemed to confirm our decision. It is interesting that three weeks after Fred announced our decision to leave UCM, Gordon announced that he, too, would be leaving, and actually left before we did.

We had a wonderful farewell from UCM. They gave us a beautiful tablecloth on which many wrote farewell words to us. The Women's Ministry gave me wooden oxen pulling a cart with one hundred little baskets tied to it; this is a miniature of what one might see along the roads -- a man going from town to town selling his wares. To top it off, they had a big grandioso fiesta farewell. Since people from about 25 different countries went to this church, the potluck included a variety of international foods. It was decorated in a very typical Filipino fiesta style. They also provided for us a container to ship all of our personal effects back to the USA. It was much bigger than we needed, so we went out and bought new furniture and pearl inlaid trunks made by the "Moros", (an Islamic ethnic group in the south) for each of the children, plus many more gifts for our friends back in the USA.

It was very hard to leave these dear people. We had spent five years ministering to them through teaching, counseling, and mentoring. It was a great time being involved in the lives of people from so many diverse cultures. I think working with so many nationalities prepared us for coming back to the USA.

Ten days before we were to fly out of the Philippines in 1991, Mt. Pinatubo Volcano erupted 60 miles north of Manila, sending ash into the city. To make matters worse, a tropical storm came along and made this ash like wet cement. Its weight on the roofs of houses began to cause them to collapse. We quickly hired some men to clean our roof from this wet ash.

Planes, however, could not take off because the ash kept piling up on the runways. We even wore masks over our noses to filter out the ash. In spite of this possible delay in our travel plans, we kept packing and praying that we would be able to fly out on time. Our plan was to take the girls through Europe on our way home to visit many places, as well as people we had met in the Philippines.

One dear family, Linda and Jim Murray, felt so bad that Debi wouldn't get to finish high school at Faith Academy that they offered to let Debi stay with them so she could finish her last two years there. But we just couldn't bear to leave her there.

God really answered our prayers. Our flight was the first one able to leave the Philippines. It left three hours late, but at least we were able to leave for the first leg of our journey. I'll tell you more about that in the next chapter.

Chapter 15
(1991-1992)

RETURNING TO USA THROUGH EUROPE
Dashed hopes turn to blessings

Through a dear friend, Danny Carreon, Fred was able to get us Business Class seats for the first leg of our journey to England. Since this was a very long flight, we really enjoyed the good meals and special services (I especially liked the foot rest).

In England, we stayed with the Gallagher's, who had been good friends of ours in the Philippines. Andy was in the Philippines to supervise Dunkin' Donuts shops in Asia. He was doing the same thing now in England and Europe. Mary and the two children welcomed us with open arms. They had rented a lovely home with plenty of space for visitors. Denise and Mary had met at the Philippine School of Interior Design.

Mary was a superb hostess and brought us all breakfast in bed. She also took Denise and Debi to a formal 3 pm high tea at a lovely hotel. I stayed home and took care of the children. The next day, Denise and Debi decided to venture out on their own to the famous Piccadilly Square. At about 3 pm, they decided to look for a place to have afternoon tea.

Finally, they saw a sign pointing to an upstairs tea parlor. This, however, had a very different kind of atmosphere. Instead of the fancy white decorated tables with waiters wearing white gloves, there was just a simple waitress wearing an apron and chewing gum. Her accent told them that she was "Cockney." She told them to sit at one of the picnic style tables. They decided to order flapjacks, thinking they were like a pancake; soon the waitress came with the cakes (not pancakes) and tea. The girls didn't like raisins, so they left them on the side of their plates. When the waitress came to give them their bill, she sat on the edge of the picnic table and began eating the raisins off of their plates as she added up their bill.

We all enjoyed their dramatization of this scenario that evening. They got a taste of "high tea" and "low tea!" They still love to act out this story -- just ask them.

While we toured around London, Fred attended a conference in Brighton on the southern coast. I got to join him the last night he was there. It was spectacular! Many of the Anglican priests had been baptized in the Holy Spirit, and freely expressed their worship to God with raised hands, dancing, and most of all joyful singing. Fred enjoyed being a part of this week-long ecumenical conference. When we revisited England in 2008, it was such a joy to see that many Anglican churches were now called "New Wine Anglican churches"—the move of the Holy Spirit in the 1980's in England has had a lasting effect on the Anglican Church.

From London, we flew to Frankfurt. We were supposed to be met by someone from Walter and Irene Heidenreich's group. We had first met this couple when they came to Manila about six years earlier. They stayed with us along with one another couple. Both of these couples had been part of a drug commune, until God spoke to them and told them to get a Bible and read it. Walter has written this amazing story and published it under the title "HELP! I NEED SOMEBODY." I highly recommend it.

Now six years later, we had the privilege to visit their ministry in Lüdenscheid. They now had a Bible School where nine of their students would be leaving the day after we arrived to start a Drug Rehab ministry in the Philippines. Fred had the privilege of joining in praying over this group and sending them out. Even though we had left the Philippines, God was calling the next generation to come and continue the task of bringing people out of bondage.

We all enjoyed being with these dear people. They took us around to see the sights, and the girls especially enjoyed the ancient castles. Years later, Debi and Brian visited this community again on their honeymoon. Walter and Irene have also come to the USA to see us.

Walter is an evangelist and travels all over Germany and other countries preaching the true message of God's love and salvation.

While in Germany we took the train to Paris. Fred had arranged a little apartment for us to stay in for a few days. We enjoyed just seeing the sites and eating the food. Next we flew to Amsterdam for a few days. I remember how much Denise and Debi enjoyed visiting the Van Gogh Museum as well as other museums there.

When we finally arrived in the USA, we were guests of Fred's Lebanese relatives in Norfolk, VA. They had a great welcoming home party for us. A couple of days later we left Denise and Debi with cousins, borrowed Cousin Buddy's big Lincoln Continental, and headed toward Maine to attend the Body of Christ Conference. We wanted to get to know these people, as we would be working in one of their communities in Minneapolis.

We were making good time when, suddenly, the traffic on the freeway on the Belt Line of Washington, D.C. came to a stop. Although we had been stopped in traffic for some time, the car behind us didn't seem to see that we were stopped and plowed into us. How we praise God that we only received minor injuries, but the car was totaled. We felt terrible about this, but Buddy said he was trying to find a way to get rid of it anyway. At least he got some insurance money out of it!

Another one of Fred's dear cousins, who worked for the FBI in Washington, D.C, offered to help us rent a car because we didn't have a credit card. After a good night's sleep at their house, we were back on the road the next day. We arrived in Maine that night just in time for the conference.

Fred and I were both experiencing a lot of body aches, probably from the impact in the accident. Two doctors attending the conference gathered a group around us to pray for our healing. This was a great introduction to this very caring, godly group of people. By the way, this was an ecumenical group of people both Catholic and Protestants. Differences in doctrine were not an issue; we just centered our lives on knowing Jesus and making Him known. I had always dreamed of being part of a community like this.

After a wonderful time together at this conference, listening to teaching, worshiping, and getting to know our new family, we took the car back to Norfolk, and then flew to California. We met up again with our daughters, who had flown there a few days before us.

The whole family was together again for the first wedding in the family. Daran cooked the dress rehearsal dinner in Lyndi's little apartment. My sister, Karen, and my mother were also there.

David and Lyndi Parshall were married August 10, 1991. Lyndi was such a beautiful bride; being the smart shopper she is, she bought this very expensive wedding dress for a very good price even though it was too big. A dressmaker did a beautiful work of art in fitting it just right for little petite Lyndi.

Fred officiated the wedding, which was held in the chapel on the Queen Mary, and the reception was at a lovely place right on the water called "The Hop."

Fred's brother, Chuck, saw that we needed a car so he gave us a 1973 Mercedes Benz. Wow! We really traveled in style! Soon we had packed the car, Daran, Denise, and Debi all in the back seat, and we headed for our new home in the Body of Christ Community in Minneapolis, Minnesota. The English Tudor house we saw and liked a year earlier had closed in Escrow and now belonged to us.

Our plan was to drive to Grand Junction, Colorado and stay with Fred's Uncle Howard and Aunt Avenell the first night; this was about a 10-hour road trip from Long Beach, CA. However, the car started giving us trouble when we were still about 4 hours from their house. It was a good thing we had Daran with us, as he knew a lot about fixing cars. But we needed a new part, so we had to drive slowly and stop often so we wouldn't overheat. We finally got there about 5 am the next day. We slept most of the day while the car was being fixed. Actually, the repair shop had to order the part, and it took a few days to finally get us on the road again. In the meantime, Aunt Avenell fed us well, and she and Uncle Howard took us around the area to see God's beautiful creation.

Two days after leaving Grand Junction, we arrived at our new home. It was great fun watching the girls plan the upstairs, which we gave to them to decorate as they pleased. The first thing they did was remove four layers of wallpaper and paint! The neighbors were quite shocked. They said the former owners had just newly wallpapered the house! To my daughters, this just wasn't their style! They wanted to paint it instead.

All the things we had shipped from the Philippines arrived a few days later. It was great having Daran there; he was such a big help, but after two weeks, he needed to get back to California and begin his last year in college. After college, Daran moved to Riverside and worked for a few years in his uncle Chuck's Benchmark Clock business. During a Merchandise Marketing Exhibit, Daran met his soon to be wife, Alicia, and moved to Raleigh, NC. He soon became the East Coast salesman for Victorinox Swiss Army Corp. He gifted all his siblings and us with sunglasses, knife sets, luggage, and various other items that he sold. After his marriage ended, he bought a small bungalow and began renovating it into a beautiful home. He also went into business with a friend of his in Foreign Car Restoration and Repairs. This business venture was very productive, but problems with the partnership soon ended this endeavor. He bought a small repair shop that was going out of business, and has turned it around into servicing and repairing high-end and foreign cars.

His next great adventure, which is still in progress, is adding a pool and 2,000-foot addition to his house. He has used well the gifts God has given him.

School was soon to start for Debi as well, who would be in 11th grade. We discovered, however, that because she was in the upper 25% in her class, she could jump right into Junior College. That's exactly what she did! She also found a part-time job at Chili's as a hostess. Denise wanted so much to get a job in Interior Design, but had to take a Department Store clerk job for the first year. She finally did land a job at Techline in Minneapolis, and spent 10 years working there in Interior Design.

I really enjoyed our time living in Minneapolis. I got deeply involved with life in the Community. I taught piano to some of the children, and trained Debi to teach beginner piano to two young students so she could earn a little extra money. I also taught a weekly Bible Study. We helped in any way we could with life in the Community.

Our next-door neighbors were the Lilly's. Their youngest of five children had Leukemia. At one point she was near death; Fred had the rare blood type that she needed and he actually saved her life by giving platelets. She is now an active teenager.

Our first snowfall came on October 31st -- 28 inches in one night! There were two more "dumps" of snow of over 20 inches each within the month. This was great fun for all of us who hadn't lived in snow as a family since 1972. But it was hard work for Fred to keep the sidewalks clean.

For Debi's 17th birthday, we got her a black Labrador that she named Marley. We took him to training school, but he flunked the first round and had to take it again. I guess he was just too playful to train.

Every Saturday night there would be a celebration of the Lord's Day -- following the Jewish tradition of preparing for the Sabbath. Three or four families would gather for a meal in one home to celebrate this beautiful ritual of honoring the Lord. Sunday mornings we attended Bethlehem Baptist Church pastored by Dr. John Piper, a well-known writer and speaker. We were so blessed! Then on Sunday afternoons, our Community would gather for worship, teaching, and fellowship.

We would help each other out with babysitting, cleaning houses when someone was sick and, most of all, just being there for one another. About 27 families lived within walking distance of each other. During the winter, we exercised together in one of the girl's basement while the little children joined in. Our daughters also enjoyed getting to know some of our neighbors like the Lilly's, the Vondracheks and the Abbotts.

But our joyful life in the Community was about to end.

Chapter 16
(1992-1994)

UNEXPECTED CHANGES
"When the going gets tough, the tough get going."

In August of 1992, we found ourselves in Vancouver, Washington looking for housing. Let me tell why we were there.

Ministering in the Body of Christ Community for the past year had been a very blessed time for me. I thought we would be staying there for the rest of our lives. But God had another plan for us.

It soon became apparent in the Community that because of the recession, the money to support four full-time workers was not sufficient. $4,000 a month was being taken from savings to keep us all on staff. It was suggested that all four full-time workers should look for part-time work.

A friend of ours, Wendell Anderson, was the director of the counseling department for the Billy Graham Association and suggested to Fred that he apply for a position in that department. There were two other options open at BGEA for Fred, including being Field Manager in the Development Department. This latter opportunity would mean that we would have to relocate. It was also an opportunity for Fred to express his pastoral skills in donor relations. If Fred were to take this position it meant we would have to relocate and leave the Community and our daughters.

This was a very sad time for me; I did not want to leave my daughters, and neither did I want to leave all these dear friends with whom I had quickly bonded during the past year. Not only that, but Fred's new job would take him out of town four days every week. Through much prayer in the Community and many prophetic words, we finally decided God was calling us to move. BGEA asked Fred to go to Vancouver, WA to be the Field Manager in Development for the BGEA in the Pacific Northwest and Alaska.

We found a very lovely house, and closed on the house in Vancouver the same day we closed on our house in Minneapolis. The girls found an apartment together in uptown Minneapolis close to a lake. Debi wasn't quite 18, so Denise became her guardian. Debi decided to enroll at the University of Minnesota in the fall. It was fun to think of Debi going there because this was my Alma Mater.

Denise got a job with the Techline Company the same day Fred began working for BGEA, August 10, 1992. She finally got the chance to put her Interior Design education and talent to use. Her specialty at this company was putting offices in homes. She was featured in the Midwest Home and Design magazine in 1994 under the title of "Midwest Design Award Winners." She also redesigned all the offices for the Chemistry Department at U of M. After spending 10 years at Techline, she moved on to another company called "Fluid Interiors." This was a wonderful change for her, as she got to use her creative skills in a multitude of new ways.

After getting through the initial grief of leaving my dear daughters, my friends, and my home, I began to seek the Lord about why I was here in Vancouver. It didn't take long for God to answer.

My next-door neighbor, Scott, was the stay-at-home partner of Bill. We became good friends. He taught me much about gardening, as we often chatted over the fence. He soon began to tell me about his life and how he got into his present lifestyle. He had a lot of sad things happen to him. I began praying for him. After about a year of friendship, one day he told me he had AIDS, and asked me, "Ruth, there isn't anything in the Bible about my lifestyle, is there?" I answered that I was so sorry about his illness, and suggested he read Romans 1:18-32. The next day as I was walking to our mailbox, Scott called out to me, "Hey, Ruth, I've been reading what you told me to read." He seemed very excited about it. Unfortunately I never saw him again. That night he took a turn for the worse and was soon on hospice care. I took flowers and a card to him and tried many times to go see him, but Bill wouldn't let me in.

I felt so bad for him and prayed daily that he was being well cared for and that he had made peace with God. One day while walking by his house, I just burst into tears wondering if he ever gave his life to Jesus. But God spoke to my mind saying, "Ruth, worry no more; Scott is with me." How comforting it is to have in us the Holy Spirit, who really consoles our hearts in times of sorrow.

Soon Debi left Denise and came to live with us! She came just in time to enter the spring quarter at Clark Community College. There was a special reason why she came: her sweetheart from Faith Academy days was living in Vancouver, B.C. -- just a day's drive away! Now she would be able to see him more often.

But the sad part is that they soon broke up, and Debi was heart-broken. She managed to still go to school each day, but she grieved very much over this loss. I felt so bad for her and decided to just read to her each night. I had found a set of all the "Little House on the Prairie" books at a garage sale, and we began reading a chapter every night. She seemed to really enjoy these books and so did I. They had always been my favorites growing up. But most of all I just enjoyed spending time with her each evening and walking with her through this grieving period; what a joy this was to have her home again!

At Clark, she soon met the love of her life -- Brian Jones. I use to tease her that she couldn't marry a Jones because he might be a relative of mine, as Jones was my maiden name. The next school year, she decided to move to an apartment of her own with other college girls while she finished up her junior college education.

Of course, we missed Denise terribly, so we decided to fly back and see how she was doing. She had prepared a great surprise for us! She took us to see the Opera, "Porgy and Bess," the first American Opera written by George Gershwin. We had a great time just being with her and seeing her enjoying her new job with the Techline Company.

We attended the New Heights Baptist Church in Vancouver, WA, and I got involved with the women's ministry. I also started a weekly worship time at our house with a few gals who were really hungering for more of God in their lives. These were very special bonding times, and we still stop to see some of them when we drive through Vancouver. There is a strong bond that seems to develop through times of worship with other like-minded people.

Fred was enjoying a very successful ministry with BGEA. He was like a pastor to the donors in the organization. His job was to help BGEA donors with planned giving, but his main ministry appeared to be to pray for and minister to them. He was doing this four days a week, but I got to have him at home three nights a week. Often I would travel with him, enjoying the blessing of staying in various hotels and not having to cook. I did get lonely at times, but I read a lot, wrote emails and, at Daran's request, wrote the first draft of my memoirs. I also had time for studying the Scriptures and prayer. BGEA would not allow the spouse to visit the homes with her husband for fear of "undue influence." Wow! I never knew I had so much power!

Fred had the opportunity to meet a number of famous people who were donors to BGEA. I loved it when he would come home telling me of the opportunities he had to pray with people and encourage them in their spiritual journey. I'll never forget one man who was very ill and wanted an ordained pastor to come and tell him how to become a Christian. Fred showed up, but he wanted to make sure Fred had the credentials of a pastor before he led him to the Lord! After Fred explained to him how to become a child of God, he also prayed for the man's healing. God is so good; he also healed the man!

Fred often visited Roy Rogers and his wife Dale in their last days on earth, and the composer, Hugh Martin, of the song, "Have Yourself a Merry Little Christmas." One time, a lady called Fred and asked him to come and help her plan her husband's funeral. At the time he wasn't expected to live, but when Fred arrived he asked if he could go see the man and pray over him. The man lived another 2 years! Fred's main purpose, of course, was to help people who wanted to put BGEA in their trusts or wills. Through this, the work of BGEA could continue to reach the world with the message of God's wonderful plan for them to have an abundant life. (John 10:10)

Each year Fred and I would get to go to the COVE, which is the BGEA Retreat Center in the Blue Ridge Mountains. This is a time when all the Field Managers (reps) from all over the USA and Canada come together. Often the wives would come too, and we had fun just hanging out, shopping, eating, laughing, and enjoying the fellowship. Each year at one of these meetings, the men were honored in the work they had accomplished the past year. One year, Fred received an award for best performance of "Essential Functions." When this was announced some people began to snicker, as this title could have meant a number of things. Soon we were all laughing heartily. Finally the director caught on, and soon they renamed the award. Fred was very effective in his work, and not only in ministering to the donors; four years in a row, he got the award for bringing in the most money.

While in Vancouver, we celebrated our 40th wedding anniversary; we decided to have a murder mystery party. Each of our children played a part in the play where we would try to discover who the murderer was. Everyone came in appropriate dress for his/her character. We would play one scene at a time after each course of the meal. We read our parts from the booklets provided; finally, we discovered "who done it!" Daran, playing the part of a hippie with a guitar, was the culprit! These murder mystery games can be a lot of fun. We had also put on similar parties in the Philippines with our friends. Debi and Denise got to serve the food. They looked so elegant in their hostess gowns.

Another great memory from those two years living in Vancouver was that my dad and his second wife, Delores, came for a visit on his 82nd Birthday. I decided to go all-out and actually put 82 lit candles on his cake. Surprisingly, a little wind blew the smoke from the candles and caused the fire alarm to go off! We all had a good laugh.

One of the great memories I had with Debi was when she and I drove down from Vancouver by way of the back side of the Sierra Nevada Mountains to Bishop, where we met Kevin, Robin, Brittney, David, and Lyndi. We enjoyed sleeping in tents in the cool mountain air, but I think David and Lyndi opted to stay in a nearby hotel. My only problem was finding the outhouse in the pitch dark; I had forgotten to bring a flashlight. The next morning, our neighbors in the next lot told us a bear had gotten into their food during the night. Then I freaked out; I could have encountered a bear! Pretty scary thought! We did see a bear the next day meandering up the hill away from us. I think it was Robin who freaked out this time!

I had grown up with a father who loved to campout, but Fred never cared much for this, so camping out with Debi near Bishop, CA was a real treat for me. Kevin and Brittney caught a fish in the little stream and we all had a taste. We hiked in the mountains and just had a great time hanging out together.

After two years in Vancouver, we applied to transfer to California, where Kevin, David and Lyndi lived. Daran also lived there and worked for Fred's brother, Chuck Sprague, at his Benchmark Clock Company.

We were going down to California for Kevin and Robin's wedding so BGEA told Fred to take the company car and visit some donors to get a "feel" for the area and see if we wanted to move there.

We spent a day with a realtor, Patti, our future sister-in-law to be, looking at houses in the Riverside area. Soon we found just the one we wanted. We went back to Vancouver and put our house up for sale. We had 30 days to sell if we wanted to get the house in Riverside. God answered our prayers, confirming our move. Again we closed on both houses at the same time in 30 days exactly!

We were so thrilled that Kevin had found the love of his life. Robin was a beautiful, red-haired bride; her daughter, 7-year-old Brittney, was the flower girl. Fred officiated the wedding as he had for all of our children. I especially enjoyed learning to do line dancing at the reception. I kicked off my fancy shoes and had the time of my life!
Driving back to Vancouver after the wedding we were filled with joy at the prospect of soon living near Daran, our two married sons, their wives, and an instant granddaughter (our first). But we were sad again to leave Debi behind; however, she had now met her life partner, Brian, at Clark College. They both graduated from Clark in 1995 and continued their education at the University of Washington in Seattle. They went on to get their postgraduate degrees at Washington State University in Pullman, Washington.

We were very blessed that the BGEA moved us from Minneapolis to Vancouver, and then to Riverside. Another new stage of life — being grandparents — was ahead for us in California.

Chapter 17
(1994-2000)

A GROWING FAMILY
"Grandchildren are the crown of life."

We soon settled into a lovely house in Riverside. The couple we bought the house from were also Christians, and had been praying for Christian people to buy the house and continue shining the light of Christ in this neighborhood. We were the answer to their prayers!

We quickly made friends with the neighbors; across the street lived an elderly retired couple. The husband was always doing beautiful woodworking projects in his garage. He kindly gave us samples of his work. Next door was a Mexican family who, we later discovered, were keeping "illegals" in their garage. Two were young boys, about 12 and 14, whose father had found work nearby. I made friends with them, so when one had a terrible toothache his brother came to me for help. I called my Christian dentist and asked if he could do some charity work. He was glad to help. Soon the boy was free of pain and we became good friends. However, it wasn't long after that the father moved them to another location. Perhaps he was afraid we would report them to the authorities.

We decided to put our roots down at the Bible Fellowship Church where Phil Busbee was the pastor. His style of preaching was expository -- where he really delved into the Scriptures -- quite different than the topical preaching so common today. We both got involved by teaching Sunday school classes. I especially enjoyed teaching the "Experiencing God" study by Henry T. Blackaby & Claude V. King. I also taught a series on mentoring and established a mentoring program in the church.

Next, the pastor asked me to head-up a Women's Ministry. This was great fun; I could really put my organizational skills to use. I developed a team of twelve -- each one was responsible for a different area of the Women's Ministry. We met together monthly for prayer, planning, and reports. I continued in this role for four years.

The one area I enjoyed the most was setting up Women's Retreats each year. The last one I led was in 1998. I asked Tommie Femrite to come from Colorado as the speaker. I had met her when she was the speaker at a Women's Aglow retreat and I taught one of the classes. Her husband was second-in-command at Clark Air Base at that time.

I'll never forget my experience at that retreat in the Philippines in 1986. I had told my class that if any needed further prayer to please let me know. One lady came to me later and asked for prayer to have a baby. She had been married eight years with no children. As I prayed for her, I had a vision of her rocking a baby; it was so real that I began to cry. I knew God was telling her she would have a child.

10 months later, when I was asked again to speak at Clark Air Base, I got to meet the fulfillment of this prophecy — a darling little boy! Since that time I have often had prophecies, but nothing that profound! God really built my faith through this experience, and I began to ask Him for more words for hurting people. He has been faithful to do that. I love hearing God speak and bring His healing touch to people. Whoever said being a Christian is boring hasn't experienced all He has for them.

The 90's were the years of marriages and grandchildren. David and Lyndi married in 1991, Kevin and Robin married in 1994, and Denise and Jason married in 1997 (they decided to end their marriage seven years later). Daran and Alicia married in 1998 (their marriage was terminated about two years later), while Debi and Brian married in 1999.

A month after we moved to California, Lyndi got pregnant. I just remember how terribly sick she was every day; she could hardly keep any food down. I was really worried about her health. But beautiful Ian Philip came into the world right on time – one week before

131

David's birthday — on June 8th. Fred was hoping they would name him Carter, the maiden name of his mother, as he was born on her birthday. Unfortunately, there was already a Carter in the neighborhood.

Now it was Kevin and Robin's turn. They had lovely little Brittney, but it was time for her to have a sibling. Eighteen months after Ian was born, Dominique Kayla came into the world. She had Kevin's dark hair and eyes -- a very beautiful child.

We had become friends with Robin's parents, Dick and Millie Kahn, and would always enjoy seeing them at every family event. Millie was a very vivacious and beautiful Jewish lady, and loved being a grandma just like me. We decided we would each babysit the new baby expected in October — each taking one day a week. Sadly, this would never be. Soon it was discovered that Millie had lung cancer, and was given only about six months to live. What a shock! We were so sad.

When Dominique was four months old, Robin had to go back to work part-time, so they asked me to come two days a week and babysit. I jumped at the chance! I would get up early Tuesday mornings and drive the 35 miles to Diamond Bar, stay overnight, and drive home again Wednesday evening. I did this for 2 ½ years and enjoyed every minute of it, even when I ran out of gas one time on the freeway at 5 am.

When Dominique was just five months old, Kevin, Robin, Brittney, and baby Dominique were gone over a weekend. When they got back to their condo, they discovered that the toilet had flooded the whole house. They had to move to a hotel for a month. It was during this time my mother came for a visit to see her new grandchildren. She stayed with me in the hotel for a night as we took care of Dominque during those two days. We spent our time caring for baby Dominque and touring around the area.

One day in March, Millie called and asked us to come visit her in Huntington Beach. She wanted us to tell her how she could know for sure that she would go to heaven when she died. Fred took the day off and we went to see her. I remember that Millie was all dressed up waiting for us. Fred explained to her that we would pray for her healing, but he couldn't guarantee that God would heal her. However, if she would believe in Jesus, he could promise her that she would have eternal life with God in heaven. He explained to her how Jesus died for her sins, and what she needed to do was believe in Him and ask Him to come and live in her heart. She said she believed and wanted to confess her sins, and to ask Jesus to accept her as one of His children. After she bowed her head and prayed, she opened her tearful eyes, and with a shining, smiling face she said, "I wanted to do this for a long time now, but I didn't know how." I thought to myself, I wonder how many other people in the world would want to know how to have eternal life, but don't know how to reach God? Fred encouraged Millie to tell others what she had done and what God had done for her.

Millie died a few months later, and Fred was asked to officiate the funeral. One of the people who spoke at the funeral was her brother, who confirmed the fact that Millie had called him and told him how she accepted Jesus into her heart. All the Jewish people in attendance got to hear that Jesus is their Messiah! We know that we shall be reunited with her in heaven. But while we're here on earth, her family constantly remembers her and lights a candle for her at every family event. Perhaps she is looking down and also enjoying being with us in spirit.

When Dominique began to talk, I taught her songs and one particular Scripture verse: "Do all things without complaining" (Philippians 2:14). She loved to sing songs as we traveled in the car. She would always ask for the "Jesus songs." One day I decided to take her back to my house to see her grandpa. Fred had hip surgery, so I needed to be there for him. She would ask to sit up on the bed by him, like she knew he needed company. When Fred was able to get back to his desk, she would go into his office and ask to sit on his lap while he worked. She seemed very content to just sit there. It was amazing how she loved being with her grandpa.

One time when we were going to my house in the van, the wind began to grow stronger and stronger. I put a cassette tape on for Dominique to be able to sing along, so she wouldn't be frightened by the wind. Soon debris was flying across the road and hitting the windows. I was going very slowly like all the other traffic and

Dominique was singing and clapping and I was joining with her. Suddenly she stopped!

I looked in the mirror and saw she had discovered all that was going on around her. Then she said, "Gamma, don't cash!" (crash) I assured her God was with us and He would take care of us. All around us trucks were off the road. The overpasses were closed. We heard later that 70 trucks had overturned. Yet we made it safely to our house in Riverside. How we thanked our God!

When Ian was about 2½, we went out to Sunday lunch with David and Lyndi. Ian told us a BIG secret -- he was going to have a baby sister! His parents had only told him they were going to have a baby; Ian added the sister part on his own! Very prophetic, because darling little Jacqueline Rose was born six months later on March 18, 1998. A few months later David got his Master's degree from UC Irvine.
In a little pink book with angels on it, I have written many of the "cute" sayings Ian, Dominique, and Jacqueline said when they were small. Let me just share one that I thought was amazing: One day when Dominique was two, I asked her where God was, and she pointed up to heaven; then I asked her where Jesus was, and she also pointed to heaven. I said, "Yes, you are right, but Jesus also lives in our hearts," and I pointed to her heart. Later I wondered why I said this to her as that is quite a deep thought for such a little one. But when her daddy came home, she climbed up on the couch next to him and said, "Know what, Daddy? Jesus lives in my heart!" Again I was amazed at how God works even in the mind of a two-year-old.

In 1999, Brian Jones and Debi Thomas were joined together in a beautiful outdoor ceremony at a lovely winery along the shoreline of the Columbia River in Oregon. Everything was ready; each of the three little attendants – Ian, Dominque, and a little girl Debi use to nanny -- had their little, silver-painted buckets with rose pedals inside, ready to be laid on the white carpet leading to the altar. Jacqueline wasn't included because she was only 15 months old, but when she saw her cousin, Dominique, with that pretty little silver bucket, she dashed up to her, grabbed the bucket and ran. Dominique burst into tears! We quickly solved the problem, but then Jacqueline was crying. Finally everyone settled down and the wedding began.

Debi was another one of those beautiful brides that should be in the wedding magazines! After the wedding, we enjoyed a reception in the dining area in the winery. Kevin, who had made up a poem about her before she was born, entitled, "I'm Going to Have a Baby Sister," composed another poem about her getting married. Every family should have a poet!

A few months later while watching TV, we heard about a prayer-walk gathering taking place in Turkey that would culminate in Ephesus. Fred insisted I go; he would pay my way! I really didn't like the idea of going alone, so I asked 20 people to pray for me that I would have a prayer partner for the trip. When I arrived in Istanbul, as I got out of the bus at the hotel, a lady walked toward me and asked in a Scottish brogue, "Are you with Global Tours?" From then on, Dr. Lesley Stewart and I were prayer partners for the eight-day trip!

We were part of a prayer-walk to the seven ancient churches mentioned in Revelation 2-3, which are part of the 10/40 window (this is the area of the world where very few people know about Jesus) that Dr. Peter Wagner (former professor at Fuller Seminary) had initiated. Christians took tours through the countries where the Christian population is very small. A total of about 5,000 Christians went on these four tours in 1993, 1995, 1997, and 1999. There is a book written about this called, "The Move of the Holy Spirit in the 10/40 Window," by Bush and Pegues.

We had 36 people from five nations on our tour bus. We would pray quietly as we walked through the tourist sites, agreeing together that God loved these people, and praying that He would send His Holy Spirit to open their eyes to the truth He had revealed through His Son, Jesus Christ. Each evening, 36 of us would meet together to pray corporately and share about their encounters that day. We also always included in our prayers our tour guide, a lovely Muslim lady. As we visited the seven churches spoken of in Revelation, she would tell us the history of these churches; she quoted more Scripture than most Christians know! She told us how she had a lot of Christian tour groups who tried to convert her and it really turned her off.

We decided we would not try to "convert" her; we would just love her. So, through small ways like buying her a cup of coffee, leaving candies on her seat, always being on time in getting on the bus, and giving her many praises, thanks, and hugs, we showed her God's love. Lesley and I had the privilege of sitting across from her on the bus one day, so we got to know her better. The next day we didn't get to sit there, but instead sat about five rows back. Just before we were ready to leave for our tour that morning, she told us how she had been sick all night. She asked if anyone else had gotten sick, but no one had. She said it was the fish we ate and she gave the restaurant manager a piece of her mind. She was still feeling badly. Then an amazing thing happened!

As she walked back, she stopped by our seats and looked at us. Lesley and I had just prayed for her that God would heal her. I looked up at her and said, "Would you like us to pray for you?" She said a hearty "YES," and I gave her my seat while I sat on the arm; she sat down between us while we prayed! God touched her, and a few hours later she came to us and told us she had no more sickness! Just more evidence that the God we love really does love us and hears us when we pray!

When our tour was over she actually cried. She said she had never had a group like ours and told us how she appreciated our being on time and not giving her any trouble. We found out later that her daughter was studying at Pepperdine University in California. I lost contact with her, but some of the others on the bus kept in contact with her for years. I prayed that she would soon become a follower of Isa (Jesus). (Do you want this last sentence to be in the past tense? Or do you want to communicate that you still pray for her to become a follower of Isa?)
On the seventh day of the tour, we ended up in Ephesus. Lesley knew missionaries in the area, the Brunson's, and I got to go along with her to their house for dinner. We had dinner with six former Muslims who were now followers of Isa. I got on email with one of them; here is his story.

Hussein worked for the Turkish government, following up people who were handicapped and receiving government aid. He was sent all over the country for his job and would quietly share the story of Jesus wherever he could. But one of his co-workers, who wanted his job, squealed on him that he was a Christian. Hussein wrote me and asked me to pray for him, as he was sure he was going to lose his job. I prayed and so did many others.

When he went in to see his boss, his boss looked at his portfolio and said smilingly, "Don't worry, Hussein, you won't lose your job; you are an excellent worker." He then told Hussein that he was the one who stood up for the Christians in another case. Perhaps his boss was a secret believer, or at least a sympathizer!

So, the 90's ended with lots of great family events as well as ministry opportunities. The future would bring another big change in our lives.

Chapter 18
(2000-2005)

PARK GRANADA
"On the move again"

We had lived in Riverside for 6 years in a lovely house with five bedrooms -- one was a "bonus" room off the garage. It was a perfect place for a piano studio. The students could enter from the garage without going into the house. I soon had about 12 students and taught most of them for about 10 years.

It was a great pleasure to see two of them, Cym and Alyssa, go on to major in piano and become proficient in their gifting. What a recent surprise it was for me to see Cym judging piano students at Ramona High School. She has really passed me up! Alyssa teaches music at a pre-school, writes worship songs, and sings as well. She and her husband are planting a church in Fontana.

But the most fun of all was teaching piano to my four grandchildren. First it was Brittney who started lessons at the age of eight. She continued lessons and was in many recitals until she was 16. One of her last recital pieces was the theme from "Ice Castles," which she played so beautifully.

Ian started lessons when he was six. He learned quickly, but struggled with rhythm; however, one would never know it today! He decided to try the trumpet and played in the school bands for three years, but his present instrument of choice is the guitar, which he plays on a worship team at his church. He also gives lessons to two guitar students. I think it's interesting that he loves the acoustical guitar so much; this is what my father, his great-grandfather, played all of his life. Ian has also been trying different sports. The ones he seems to love the most presently are long-boarding and mountain biking.

Dominique started lessons when she was 4 ½. When Robin told me the pre-school was offering piano lessons to students, I also offered to start her in lessons. I wasn't about to let someone else teach MY granddaughter! She studied for about six years, but Dominique's passion is more in sports. She presently loves soccer, volleyball, track, and basketball. Time will tell as to which one will become her first love.

When Jacqueline was three, I decided to see what she could learn on the piano by rote. I soon discovered she could learn a lot! At 3½ she was in her first piano recital. She was so shy that she asked Brittney to come up and sit on the piano bench with her as she played. But it wasn't long before she was enjoying performing. Whenever the family would get together, I would have the children play, and as an added incentive they also got points toward a prize if they played for anyone during the week.

At present, she plays keyboard on a worship team at church. The style of keyboard playing on a worship team has changed considerably over the years. Now the keyboard player basically is playing the chords that match the melody. She really taught herself to do this very effectively. She also played the bass clarinet in the honors band in sixth grade. But, I believe her greatest love in the arts is dancing — tap, jazz, ballet and especially lyrical dancing. Lyrical dancing allows her to choreograph her own dances. I love to watch how she expresses the mood of the music so gracefully.

It's been such a joy to live close to our grandchildren and watch them develop their interests, skills, and characters; we have been very blessed.

Starting a new century led to many changes in our lives. We decided that it was time to "downsize.' We found our future home listed in the newspaper and checked it out, but the owner wanted $20,000 cash to put down on a condo she was buying in Las Vegas and she wanted it quickly. Our house was up for sale and in escrow, so we thought this would be easy; however, on my birthday, May 1st, as I was praying I got this sinking feeling that this deal would not go through. I felt the Lord asking me to give up the condo idea. I guess I just loved it too much and needed to surrender it to His will. True enough, the deal did not go through. I was heartbroken, but kept surrendering it to God knowing that His will is always right and better. Soon a buyer came along, and our house was in Escrow again. We decided to go see if the condo had sold or if there were other places for sale in Park Granada. To our amazement, the condo was still available! And, as they say, the rest is history.

After moving into the condo in June, Fred and I went to Amsterdam for three weeks as volunteers to help with the Billy Graham "Amsterdam 2000" -- a conference inviting over 10,000 pastors and Christian workers from mostly third world countries to come with all expenses paid. The goal was to bless these dear workers in God's Vineyard and let them sit at the feet of some of the well-known evangelists and spiritual leaders of our time.

BGEA rented two huge coliseums, with one intended to house most of the people. They had to build showers and make cubicles with four bunks in each – a very big job! The other complex was the dining area, classrooms, and stadium for the 10 plenary sessions. My job was to be the hostess at one of hotels where we stayed. We only had about six couples, which made it fairly easy, but I also helped change the earplugs for about 4,000 attendees after each session. Each of the sessions was translated into 29 languages; this is why the earphone plugs had to be changed after every session. Fred had many jobs, such as picking people up at the airport, being an usher for the sessions, and fulfilling any other needs.

My favorite speaker of the 10 plenary sessions was Ann Graham Lotz -- the only female speaker! My second choice was the son of one of the five martyrs in Ecuador in 1957. He spoke as well as translated for the tribal man who had killed his father. The tribesman had become a Christian, and broke down crying and asking forgiveness from the 10,000 people attending this gathering. Then the son said, "How many of you people are in the ministry today because of those who were martyred in 1957?" I would guess about 5,000 people stood up. It's so true, "Nothing is going to stop the gospel from being preached." The more Christians are persecuted, the stronger the church grows.

While still in Amsterdam, I took a break from my work one day and walked over to a nearby park. There I sat on a bench to read my Bible and to pray for strength. Sitting on the bench next to mine, I noticed a young man reading his Bible and praying. About 40 minutes later, he got up and walked past me. He turned around when I called out to him, "Are you visiting here to attend the Billy Graham Convention?" He came over and we began to talk; he was in Amsterdam leading a worship team for the Campus Crusade Conference, but said he would really like to attend the Convention. I said I would try to get him a ticket, which I did. But as we sat and talked, I was drawn to this young man and felt God wanted me to pray for him and his future.

We have been in contact ever since. I prayed for a wife who would be a true partner for him in ministry; God answered that prayer a few years later. As for his ministry, Joel Rajkumar soon left Campus Crusade and is now an evangelist traveling widely throughout India. We were able to host him one of the times he came to the USA to speak. I am always so amazed at the hand of God -- how he leads us day by day and gives us such exciting encounters if we just open our eyes, our mouths, our hearts, and our ears!

After we left Amsterdam, we stopped in Scotland to see Lesley and her family. (If you remember, Lesley was my prayer partner on the trip to Turkey.) She invited us to come to Aberdeen. She and her husband lived in a quaint, 100-year-old house with narrow stairways and a tiny bathroom (at least it had indoor plumbing). But they had built a separate little prayer room where Lesley spent much time and also had small groups come to pray. The big picture window, which took up all of one side of the room, overlooked the beautiful garden and hills. God certainly gave me the very best companion for my trip to Turkey!

Lesley and Doug had arranged for us to stay one night at the Kilravock Castle built in 1130. The Countess who lived there was a Christian and decided to turn her castle into a type of "bed and breakfast." It was great fun exploring this castle, climbing up on the roof and the lookout tower. I can imagine many wars were fought from there.

After this week, Lesley and Doug took us by train to Edinburgh, where we saw the amazing Military Tattoo production. I sat spellbound for two hours. The horsemen rode out of the castle in a cloud of smoke toward the field where the program took place. Dancers and bands from all over the British commonwealths performed for the next two hours. It's a must-see for anyone traveling there.

We also went to St. Andrews for a few days. We had heard about this famous fish restaurant an hour away on the coast, and decided to take the crowded bus there to experience eating this special fish. When we finally got there, we were surprised to see it was just a little café right on the ocean, and the line waiting to get in was about 15 feet long out the door. When we finally got our food, it was served on a paper plate like a fast-food place in the USA. The fish was deep-fried and the chips were served with a vinegar dip; it was definitely a new experience for us.

Since the days when we lived in Vancouver, WA, I had been attending the Christian Renewal Center (CRC) in a beautiful forest area near Silverton, OR. My friend, Chris Piper, and I would go there occasionally for a spiritual "getaway." When we moved to Riverside, I flew back there and took Brittney with me for three summers. One of those times she took a friend with her. Years later when this friend graduated from college, she thanked me for taking her to the camp. She told me that it had significantly impacted her life.

Debi was now living on her own while going to school at Clark Community College in Vancouver, WA. She also was working for Vista, an organization like the Peace Corps. She worked under Chris Piper in a very under privileged area. Debi wrote a grant to get funds for a summer camp for these kids. She got the money two summers in a row and ran the camp herself! I'm sure many children who probably never would have had a chance to attend a summer camp enjoyed this experience.

When she got engaged to Brian, she met me at CRC for one night. While she was there, she told me later she had prayed that Chris would find a husband. Three weeks later, Chris met David, the man she would marry. Chris was about 40 at this time and had been raising her son, Luke, alone. David was also a schoolteacher. After they dated a few times, she decided to invite David to CRC for the Thanksgiving weekend. Many friends were telling her not to do this since he wasn't a Christian. She called me and asked my advice. After a quick prayer for wisdom, I said, "I don't see anything wrong with you taking him to CRC; who knows, God may just touch his heart." That's exactly what happened! They have been married now for about twelve years. It was so great to see how God answered Debi's prayer again.

One year, Fred was asked to be the main speaker (I helped a little as well) at CRC. We invited our friends, Todd and Pam Volker, and their two children, Joel and Bethany, to come along and help us. I think Brittney was 14, Joel was 13, and Bethany was 10. After our week at the camp, we decided to rent two cars and drive up to Vancouver, BC for another week's vacation.

The three kids had a great time together, either all riding with us or with Pam and Todd.

We were almost to the border when Fred had an emergency, and we had to turn off and quickly look for a gas station. Todd and Pam tried to follow us, but lost us. We had said that if we lost each other we should wait at the next rest area. Unfortunately, the rest area they agreed on was only located on the other side of the freeway. At every rest stop we left a message for them. Finally, we got to the border and waited, thinking that eventually they would come. We all prayed; suddenly Bethany remembered she had her cell phone in her purse and tried to call her mother. (Pam had just turned her cell phone on!) Fortunately, she caught her parents just as they were about to take a different route to the border and cross into Vancouver at a different place than where we were. We really felt this was another answer to prayer.

We were both staying at different places in Vancouver and didn't know where each other were staying. After reconnecting, we enjoyed each other's company while touring the sites and eating fish at a café down on the boardwalk. Probably our favorite tour site was the Butchart Gardens on Victoria Island. Soon our time together was over; Fred and Brittney traveled back to Portland and then flew home, staying overnight at the lovely home of Dr. Keith and Florice Knopf, our life-long friends.

My best friend all through school, Jeannie, flew out to Vancouver from Michigan and met me there. Jeannie and I were going on the Holland America Lines cruise ship to Alaska for a week, leaving the next day after Fred and Brittney left.

Then tragedy struck. I got a call from my sisters that my mom had a stroke and was in the hospital. They had been trying to find me for days, and finally caught up with me in Vancouver the day before we were scheduled to board the ship. I was in a quandary as to what to do. Should I forfeit my cruise? I was more concerned, however, about Jeannie; she had saved her money for months to buy an airline ticket to Vancouver and to pay for the cruise. I doubted that she would go on without me. I prayed and got more details about my Mom. Lois finally helped me decide; she said Mom wasn't at death's door and felt I should go ahead with my plans. My siblings, five in all, could handle the situation. I really commend them for taking care of everything.

When I finally got to go to Michigan to visit Mom, she was in a nursing home. I tried to visit her as often as I could fly to Michigan from California. My brother, Nate, really took charge of everything. They found a nursing home quite close to his house. He had now retired from teaching school and was a professional piano Jazz musician who also taught private lessons, so he had more spare time for watching over Mom.

But it was very hard to see Mom in this state. She had a hard time communicating and called things by the wrong names; for instance, a dress, to her, was a plate. But after a while, we came to understand what she was saying. This was an extremely difficult year for all of us. It was especially hard when it was decided that she could never live back in her apartment on her own again. Lois and Karen helped her pack up her things, or give them away. I understand it was a very tearful time. I wasn't there because it was something that had to be done quickly and they didn't have time to wait for me to come.

Seeing her in the nursing home just broke my heart. I thought maybe I could find a better place for her, but Medicaid would only pay for nursing homes, and this was the best one available. Every time I came to see Mom, she would ask me to take her home with me. I seriously considered it, but everyone felt it was better for her to stay in Michigan, where more of the family could share the responsibilities. So all I could do was take her out to eat when I was there (her favorite food was a trout dinner), and try to show her my love; it really was emotionally hard.

I was planning another trip there to see her, and already had my ticket for September 21st. I decided to call her on September 8th to tell her I was coming. She was having a very hard time that day, and told me not to waste my money. On September 11, 2002, she got up and went to the dining room for breakfast; she then went back to her bed and died. I really think she died because life no longer had meaning for her.

Fred and I came a week later, as did all of our children, to say our final goodbyes to Mom, Grandma, and Great-grandma. Karen suggested I play a piano solo at her funeral. When I found out they had no piano, only an organ, I just recorded Debussy's "Clare de Lune." Later I found out it was Mom's favorite piece! It seems God was guiding me even in this small detail.

After the funeral, Fred and I went to my Uncle Nyle's place on a lake to see all my Jones relatives. Since my parents were divorced, none of them attended the funeral. Debi opted not to go and stayed at the hotel catching up on her schoolwork. Fred flew home alone, because he had to get back to work. My friend, Jeannie, offered to spend the next week with me revisiting our roots.

We went up to Gitchee Gumee Bible Camp to see Uncle Eldon and Cousin Mel, who runs the camp. Then Jeannie drove me through Stanton, where my parents grew up and where I was born. I had so many fond memories of visiting my grandmas and cousins there. We also went back to our childhood homes and school again. It was a wonderful thing she did for me. She just knew I needed this time to reminisce and to grieve over this deep loss. We had a great time together for a whole week. No one could have a better friend!

Fred was doing very well as a Field Manager for Billy Graham. He was truly a pastor to the donors as well. In 2005, his reward was to work in Alaska for a month and take me along. I had to pay my own plane fare and food, but lodging was free. The cruise I went on with Jeannie to Alaska never got to the mainland, so I got to see the real Alaska mainland when I went with Fred.

My favorite place was Denali National Park. We took a bus back into the park (you can't drive there) and saw reindeer, moose, bear, a red fox, and the famous 22,000-foot Mt. McKinley. We actually got to see the top of it, as it was a rare clear day. Near Anchorage, we took a helicopter ride and landed on a glacier. At one point the pilot saw a bull moose running in the brush below and spooked the animal. It was fun chasing him.

We also met up with Karen Backlund, an old friend from Bethel days. We liked her parents so much that we had asked them to be the guardian of our children in case something happened to us when we first went to the Philippines.
Karen loves it in Alaska. She lives in Palmer, an hour north of Anchorage, and is a social worker there. We spent the night at her house and she toured us around the area. Among other places, she took us to a musk ox farm.

After this, we went to Whittier, which is a hidden town through a tunnel -- the western gateway to Prince William Sound. The US had 4,000 troops hidden there during WW II. The barracks are still there. We got on a small launch, which held about 150 people. How surprised we were to meet up with old friends on this ship from Ligaya in the Philippines!

It was great hearing about all the amazing things God was doing in a ministry they had started called, "Couples for Christ." They told us there were, at that time, over a million members of this group! Often I have seen a bumper sticker that says, "Couples for Christ".

We got to see a lot of the mainland of Alaska during that month that Fred was working there. Meeting the people and understanding more about the "last frontier" gave me a new love for these hardworking, yet happy people. This was truly an experience I will never forget.

Chapter 19
(2003-2010)

FAMILY HIGHLIGHTS
God Blesses What He Possesses

In 2003, our whole family went to the Boundary Waters between Minnesota and Canada. We rented three condos for all of us for four days. My favorite experience was canoeing across the lake and down the river; in some places it was too shallow, so we had to get out of the canoe and carry it over the shallow or dry areas. I also remember that Ian was about eight years old, and would fish off the back of the canoe on our way back to our condo. He actually caught 10 fish —more than anyone else!

Also in 2003, we went to the Vineyard Asia Conference in Thailand. We spent a week touring a city north of Bangkok called Chiang Mai. I even took a class in how to cook Thai Food! But perhaps our greatest experience was having dinner at the home of the Eubanks, who lived about an hour away from the river that divides Thailand from Myanmar. Their mission was to help the Karen people, who were being slaughtered; their homes burned, they were forced to live in the jungle.

As we were eating dinner at their house, the phone rang. It was the captain of the boat saying they would have to change their meeting place, as the Myanmar soldiers were all around and shelling the area. That very night the Eubanks, with their two little children on their backs, met the boat, taking along a dentist to care for the teeth of the Karen people. Sometimes they would take a doctor or nurse as well. They would stay in the jungle with

148

the Karen's for three months at a time, helping them develop community life and bringing them hope and blessings.

The second week in Thailand, we were back in Bangkok for the Vineyard Asian Summit church leaders' conference, where six different nations were represented. In 2007, we would again attend a Vineyard Asia Conference — this time in Bali, Indonesia; but now 20 nations were represented with about 340 delegates. How God had blessed the missions' outreaches of the Vineyard! There are now over 700 churches abroad—more than in the USA! It has been such a joy for us to be part of this mission.

In 2006, Debi got her Individual Interdisciplinary doctorate degree from Washington State, located in Pullman. This is a small town, so it was virtually impossible to get a motel room during graduation time. Debi suggested we not come to her graduation, but instead come a week later to their home in Seattle for a big party. We decided, however, to surprise her. My cousin, Jane, lives one hundred miles from Pullman, so I asked if we could stay there.

I was sure Debi had found out about our plan, because she called me on the day we started out on our long drive and asked me where I was! Fortunately, we were still within the LA area, so I told her the truth. After that I decided I wouldn't answer her calls, as I was afraid I would give away our plan! Fred is better at covering up (without lying) than I am!

We drove all the way to my cousin's place in Coeur d'Alene, Idaho, arriving the day before the graduation. On Saturday, we drove to Pullman in time to watch the graduates march in. Brian, her husband, knew we were there, but he kept it a secret.

We were sitting in the balcony on the very side above where she was seated down on the floor by the platform. I kept praying she would look up, and soon she did! I began waving; when she saw us she burst into tears. I saw the man in front of her turn around and give her his handkerchief. She told us later that she had just said to herself, "Oh, I wish Mom and Dad were here to see this!"

And there we were! What joy we all had celebrating this very special day together!

We spent the next week traveling up to Banff, Alberta to enjoy the beauty of the mountains and Lake Victoria. We arrived back in Seattle the following Saturday just in time for the big Graduation Party, where all of her siblings flew in to be there for this momentous occasion. Our gift to her was our second car, so we put the keys to the car in a gift bag with a note. She couldn't figure it out at first; then the light went on, and she was delighted to have a car to drive to work instead of a borrowed old truck.

In 2006, Fred decided to retire from the Billy Graham Evangelistic Association. Our children gave him the very best retirement party one could imagine. They rented the Santa Barbara Room at the famous Mission Inn in Riverside, and had the food catered. About 50 people came to celebrate this momentous occasion.

As our friends and family greeted us and were seated, the former pastor of our church in Manila, Dr. and Mrs. Alex Adonis, arrived; this was a great surprise to us because he lives in Ohio. All of our children immediately got up and surrounded them with hugs and fond words of welcome. We were so honored to have them come.

After our tasty pasta dinner, Fred was honored by many "well-wishers" in attendance. But the finale happened when Daran unveiled a picture of a 1969 midnight blue Mercedes Benz 280SL convertible as he made a speech. He had been refurbishing this car for two years, putting in all new parts. What a beauty! He chose this car particularly because he was born in 1969. We would finally get to see the car at Christmas in 2007. In March of 2008, we flew to Raleigh and picked up the car for a 4,500-mile trip to its new home in Riverside. But I will tell you more of this trip later.

In July of 2006, the family was invited to the wedding of our daughter, Denise, and Craig Alamode. The day before the wedding we all enjoyed a fun day at the park. We were divided into teams to play games so we could get to know each other's families. One of the games was a relay. They later asked each one of the teams various questions about Denise and Craig and their courtship. I remember one question was: "Where did Craig take Denise on their first date?" I was the only one who knew the answer – to church!

The beautiful wedding was held in the yard of Craig's house in St. Louis Park, MN. Denise came down the little hill on the side of their house in her beautiful gown, walking to the music played by a violinist. Craig's sister-in-law, who is a professional opera singer, sang "The Lord's Prayer." Fred and Craig's pastor brother tied the knot, and we all enjoyed a time of dancing and feasting. The only problem was that the temperature went up to 105 degrees, and Denise got sunstroke from dehydration. She spent the night in the hotel, sleeping on top of the sheets and with Craig putting ice on her to bring down her temperature. She was fine the next morning when the family met for breakfast and opening gifts. We were so happy to have Craig join our family. He is 6'7", handsome, and very humorous. He loves all kinds of outdoor sports, and has accomplished the feat of becoming an Ironman. Recently he and Denise went to France, where Craig completed the Paris-Brest-Paris cycle event. 6,000 men and 200 women participated. They had to complete this event within 90 hours. Craig did it in 88. Yeah, Craig!

In November of 2006, we flew to Raleigh and picked up a Citroen car
Daran borrowed for us for our next trip. On our way to Pennsylvania we had a little car trouble. After we filled up with gas, we had to push the car to get it started again; men would come over to look at the car at the gas stations, and then help push the car so we could start it. It always amazes me how God provides all we need for every situation. Daran had the part we needed delivered overnight, so a day later we were able to continue our trip on to New York City.

In just two days in New York, we did it all. Some of my favorite things were taking a carriage ride through central park, attending a live performance of "Phantom of the Opera," and also visiting Ellis Island, where Fred's grandparents entered this country from Lebanon.

Next we drove to Washington D.C. to visit the center of government of our great country. Here we stayed with old friends, Dr. Bill Dickerson and his artist wife, Eunhee. We visited the art studio where many of her paintings are displayed. They have two musically talented children. In their living room are a Steinway Grand Piano and a harp (and not much else). They truly value music and art more than other material things.

Then we continued on to Norfolk, VA, to visit Fred's Lebanese side of the family. The cousins had a big party for us and we enjoyed getting to know these very fun-loving people. We have tried to stop and see them anytime we are in the general area.

In March of 2007, Fred and I flew to Daran's in Raleigh so we could take a few more trips along the East Coast. Daran borrowed the Citroen car for us again, and we drove first to Charleston to see our old friends, the Martins, whom we had met in the Philippines. Then we drove to Amelia Island and met Daran, along with his employees who worked on the Antique cars in his business. We attended the famous Concur d' Elegance antique car show. I would liken it to a women's fashion show, only instead of clothes, they are parading their beautiful antique cars while someone is narrating, telling all about the car and the owner. Quite a show!

After a couple of days there, we drove back to Raleigh and then flew to Europe for another great experience: visiting old friends, and five different countries. We arrived in London in the early morning on March 15, 2007; after we dropped our luggage at the hotel, we got on a "hop-on, hop-off" tour bus around the city, stopped off at the pier, and took a short tour cruise on the Thames River. It was a beautiful sunny day (I understand they don't get many of these in London). We enjoyed meeting and talking with local people, who provided us with the best inside information. Our thanks go out to Debi and Denise, who provided this Grand Tour.

The next day, we took about a seven-hour train ride to the most northern town of Wales, Liandudno, and stayed at a B&B. I had always wanted to go to Wales to see the country of my grandfather Jones' descendants. As we walked around the beautiful little town right on the ocean, we stopped at a card shop where I bought birthday cards for each of our children written in Welsh. I wanted a translation of the cards, so I asked an elderly lady. I also asked her if she knew any Joneses. She laughed and said, "Did you know that during the War, when the men from Wales signed up to serve, there were so many Joneses that they had to also go by numbers?" So I decided it probably was useless to try to find out about my descendants.

At breakfast the next morning, the hostess of the B&B was trying to open a bottle of ketchup for Fred; as she shook it, it suddenly burst open and sprayed Fred with ketchup. He had to take off all his clothes, and the lady washed and dried them while we waited.

Soon Tim and Sarah Coleman picked us up and drove us to Kendall, where we would spend the weekend. The next day they took us on a tour of the ancient city of Chester, together with Tim's father, who was our historical guide. We walked on footbridges built in the 4th century. I always enjoy visiting historical sites and this was the best, since we had a very seasoned Englishman to be our tour guide.

It was so much fun reconnecting with Sarah again. She had just become a new believer when she was with us in Manila. And now we were reconnecting and meeting her husband and four children: twin boys, 16, Anaka (a beautiful singer), 13, and Lucy, 10 at the time. It was also quite a treat that Sunday to attend their Anglican Church, which is one of many New Wine Anglican Churches in the UK today, very much influenced by the Vineyard. Truly, this is a beautiful mix of tradition and freedom in the Spirit. After a lovely Sunday dinner, we were taken to the beautiful area of the 10 Long Lakes of Windemere. It actually snowed—first snow of the year—this is the most popular vacation spot for the local Englanders.

The following day, we took the 3-hour train ride back to London to catch our plane for Rome. When we arrived in

Rome, it was raining and snowing. We were so thankful for an American student who interpreted for us, found us a taxi, and gave us many suggestions about what to see and do. Of course, we also had our trusty Rick Steeves tour guidebook.

Well, the first thing Rick says in his book is, "Rome is crazy, but the system works." We saw this at the hotel — there was no order as everyone pushed in to get their food. But we finally got our food, and so did everyone else, with a lot of happy chatter and laughter. A lady from Spain joined us at our table, and said she was on a tour to see the Pope – precisely our plan for the day as well. After two train rides and lots of walking, we arrived at the Vatican with about 5,000 other people. Fred had made contact with Fr. Raniero Cantalamessa, the pastor of Pope John Paul 23rd, who made arrangements for us to get tickets to get into the audience seating area.

After about a two-hour wait, Pope Benedict XVI arrived touring through the crowd in his "Pope-mobile." It's amazing -- it even climbs the stairs up to the podium from where he spoke. We had good seats because of the connections Fred had made. The ceremony lasted 3½, hours with the Pope's message being translated into four other languages. He spoke mostly to the youth who had come from all over the world. Children sang and played instruments. It was an awesome experience. Did you know that the Vatican is the smallest country in the world? After this we went to St. Peter's Basilica — words fail me to describe this, the largest Cathedral in the world.

The next day we visited the Coliseum, where Christians were thrown to the lions for believing in Jesus Christ. It just made me so grateful that they were willing to stand up for their faith because, if they had not, perhaps we would never have had the opportunity to know Jesus today.

There is so much to see in Italy, and the people are so friendly and vivacious. We loved the pizza — it tastes so different than pizza in the USA. Every afternoon we treated ourselves to Italian ice cream (spumoni)! Yummy!

We saw too many sites to mention here, but I must mention the Pantheon, a huge temple built in the 3rd century B.C. The dome is 142 feet high and wide. The center of the dome is completely open, so when it rains, there are drains 142 feet below in the marble floors. In later years, architects used this method for building domes. It was first built to honor the Roman gods; later it became a monument to Mary, the mother of Jesus, and the martyrs.

We also walked on the Spanish Steps and enjoyed hanging out at the Fount of Trevi, from which the song, "Three Coins in the Fountain" was written. There is so much more to tell, but let's move on to our next stop, Florence, and the Leaning Tower of Pisa. Again, it's hard to describe beautiful Florence with all its sculptures and art museums. My favorite was to see the Uffizi Art Museum.

Venice is so amazing — it's basically a city built on water, so everything floats. Some buildings have been there for a 1,000 years and are now condemned, but are still standing for the tourists to see as they pass by in small commuter boats — the only way one can travel in this city.

The Jewish ghetto of Venice was very interesting and sad to me. These people were kept on an island, and could not go over the bridges at night. They had to keep building higher and higher as their families expanded. They could not build outside of this small area. We visited the synagogue Yeshiva Gedolah Lubavitch of Venice. This Jewish ghetto was established in 1516. How God's "chosen people" have suffered throughout history!

Our next stop was Austria. After settling in at our hotel, we bought the 24-hour pass for the "hop-on, hop-off" city tours. We took all three tours, so we really got to see a lot in one day. We went to the famous Schoenbrunn Palace and attended a concert in the very room where Mozart performed. The acoustics were fabulous. We also found the house where our dear friend, Lucy Ashwall, lived until she escaped with her mother and brother from Hitler when she was 17.

The last weekend of our trip was truly the highlight. Nothing compares to the Swiss Alps and such beautiful people. We left Vienna early Friday morning by train. Daran met us about 6 pm in Lucerne; it was so good to see his handsome, smiling face and someone who spoke English. He took us by another train to the beautiful city of Stans, which has a population of about 65,000. The Engel Hotel, where we stayed for three nights, was situated amid snow-capped mountains and lovely Swiss Chalets. All this beauty was so close, it felt like we could reach out and touch it.

The next day, we met friends of Daran who were like his "Swiss family" when he often came to Switzerland for business. They entertained us royally. Daran also took us on a cruise around the huge Lake Lucerne so we could really see more of the beauty of this area.

On Sunday two of our friends, who lived a few hours away, came to see us. We got to know these two lovely ladies when they were also working in Manila with the YWAM mission. Franzi and Daniella took us to Mass at a very beautiful church. It was Palm Sunday, so they had a special service with the Passion of Christ read from the gospels. We followed along in our English Bibles. Afterwards, we had lunch together and a great time reminiscing about our times together in the Philippines.

Later in the afternoon, we took a long walk around the city with Daran's friends, Karen, Leo, and their children. That evening, we were again invited for dinner at their home. It was such a delightful evening talking with them and their parents. Fortunately, Karen was able to be our interpreter.

In reflecting back on our time in Switzerland, I realized how much I enjoyed being part of the life of one family that represented the lifestyle of most people. They were so amazed that our Thomas family is spread all over the USA, and asked if that was typical of the US. Family means everything to them. Sundays are family days – stores are closed, and people are out walking with their family and greeting one another. It reminds me of the small town my grandparents lived in and where I was born — Stanton, MI. I love the small-town atmosphere.

Well, our journey was awesome; we will never be the same. We learned so much about the history in the development of Europe, as well as how people live there today. We enjoyed the delicacies of each country: fish and chips in Wales; pizza and gelato in Italy; Wiener schnitzel and apple strudel in Austria; cheeses and chocolate in Switzerland. But most of all, we enjoyed the people we met along the way. They gave us so much. We are so thankful to Daran, who provided the air miles plus some of the other expenses so we could make this fabulous trip.

Christmas of 2007 was hosted by Daran in Raleigh, NC. It was so much fun having the whole family together again. Everyone helped make it the best, for example, by hanging handmade stockings for every person there, and with the fabulous dinner prepared mostly by Daran, Denise, and Debi. But the greatest thrill was when Debi and Brian announced they were expecting their first child! We all ran out and bought gifts for the new baby. I remember Fred buying a little basketball set. No matter what sex the baby was, it would certainly want to play basketball!

Debi was due around June 23rd, so I asked her when she wanted us to come up. She said she preferred we come after the baby was born, so she suggested June 30th. How surprised we were that she was still pregnant when we arrived. The pastors of the Vineyard church, Karl and Gail Neils, graciously opened their home to us to stay for as long as we needed.

We enjoyed four days with Debi, buying plants and deciding on what tree to plant as a welcome gift for the baby. Debi chose two blueberry bushes. But in the middle of the third night, I had a terrible nightmare that Debi's baby died in the birth canal. I was so frightened that I got up and pleaded with God to save our grandchild. After about an hour of pacing the

158

floor, crying out to God, I finally had peace and went back to bed and to sleep. In the morning I told Fred and Pastor Karl about the dream. They promised also to pray. On July 3rd, Debi went into labor. They preferred a home birth with a midwife, and Brian was right there supporting Debi all the way. But finally, after about 20 hours of labor, they felt the baby was in distress and called an ambulance to take Debi to the hospital. They immediately performed a C-section. In the meantime, Brian had called us and asked us to come over to their house to take care of the animals.

We waited for about three hours, but didn't hear anything. Finally I could stand it no longer and drove myself to the hospital. I found her room and softly knocked on the door. A nurse came out and I heard Debi say, "I don't want to see anyone yet." Then she asked who it was; when she heard it was her mother, she let me in. The baby had just been born, and they were still weighing her. Later the doctor came in and told me, "Debi could not push the baby out because she was trying to come out shoulder first." I know God intervened and little Mia Grace was born healthy and beautiful in every way. I got to be there right after the birth. This was very special for me.

When Zoe Kristine was born almost three years later, Debi was able to have a natural childbirth! We were so thrilled to get the phone call on April 4, 2011, that both mother and baby were doing well. About 10 days later, I flew to Seattle and Denise came from Minnesota to enjoy being part of this little family for a few days, in addition to helping out when we could. Denise was thrilled that Zoe had been given her middle name. I knew how much this meant to her because Denise wanted to hold her all the time; I had to wait patiently for my turn.

Fred took Jacqueline a few weeks later to Seattle to see her new cousin and to learn how to be a good babysitter. Fred really bonded with Mia, as he spent a lot of time playing with her.

Each of our children is so unique; my joy has been watching them grow and try different things. I noticed that at a very young age, David would always line things up and put things in order. Even his drawings had straight lines and he always colored inside the lines. My father was a designing engineer as well as my brother and many others in my family. Perhaps, I thought, David would be one too. At first, David was interested in architecture, but soon changed his interest to building roads and bridges.

But he also uses his skills to do a lot of renovation in their home — like putting in a completely new and beautiful kitchen. He has also done a couple of big projects for us. He, Ian, Jacqueline, and Fred tiled our back patio a few years ago. As I sit out there daily, I remember all their hard work and thank God for this gift. In 2008 we began thinking about giving our kitchen a face-lift. After getting estimates, we realized we really couldn't afford to do this. David jumped in and offered to do all the labor, if we bought the cupboards. Kevin, Ian, and even Jacqueline all helped. Jacqueline's favorite part was tearing out the old kitchen. Every day I enjoy working so much more in this lovely new kitchen. Then for Christmas, Kevin and David's families gave us a very elegant new kitchen faucet that really does the beautiful cabinets justice.

Kevin, our eldest son, has skills and interests in many different areas than our other children. One of these is the Rotary Club. One of his many responsibilities is to help man the Rotary booth at the annual LA County Fair, where they raffle off a sports car each year to raise money for their various charities. He has often led their worship services at the leadership camps sponsored by the Rotary each year for potential leaders from local high schools, and has also taught some leadership classes.

For the past 20 years, he has worked at the Forest Lawn Memorial Parks. A couple of years ago, it was discovered that seven of the co-managers with Kevin had been found guilty of fraud, and were immediately dismissed. One day the new director asked Kevin to come in and see him the next day. Kevin called us for prayer, as he was afraid that they had found something amiss among his employees as well, and that he also would be fired. But when he walked into the director's office, he was greeted with a smile and these words: "Kevin, I've been watching you carefully for the past three months and I like your style." Handing him an envelope, he said, "And I just want to give you this bonus to show my appreciation." I think Kevin actually cried, especially when he opened the envelope and found $20,000! God truly honors those who honor him. Besides the fact that Kevin shows his integrity in his work, he has always tithed his income. God made a promise in Malachi that "if you will bring your whole tithe into the storehouse, so that there may be food in My house, I will open the windows of heaven and pour out for you a blessing until it overflows." God is true to His Word.

We have been privileged to be the grandparents of Brittney, who was seven when Kevin married her mother, Robin. On November 15, 2008 Brittney became the wife of Tony Mandella. They had been sweethearts since they were 16 and 17. After high school, they continued on to college and both graduated from Azusa Pacific University. I really admire their purposeful planning for their lives.

At their wedding shower, I said something to the effect that, "no wedding is perfect and it's usually the unusual imperfections that make the wedding so memorable." Well this wedding tops the charts! The very night of their beautiful wedding in Newport Beach the worst fire anyone in the Inland Empire could remember broke out. The freeway, Highway 91, was closed because the flames were so intrusive. Fortunately, most of us had already moved to a hotel near the wedding event, and didn't have to try to find a way around the fire. Guests, however, had to travel as much as four hours longer to get to the wedding. We started a little late, but it was a beautiful wedding, especially the bride. Fred had the joy marrying our first grandchild.

The next big event in our family was a trip to the Philippines in 2009. Not everyone could go, but Kevin, David, and Debi's families went with us. Fred and I went a week ahead so we could also visit Cebu City, where we had lived and worked for 20 years. We stayed at the old mission guesthouse. We invited anyone who wanted to see us to come there.

Among those who came were our fabulous household helper, Ester, and her husband, Boy. They are not well, but made the three-hour bus trip from the North to come and see us. Many members from the church we started in this city also came to thank us for coming. One man whom we did not recognize thanked us profusely for bringing the truth of God's love and His salvation for all who believe to his grandfather. Because of this, generations later, his whole family are believers in Jesus, and this young man is now the assistant pastor of the church we started there about 35 years ago. What a joy for us to live long enough to see this fruit of our labor!

After our visit in Cebu, we flew back to Manila and stayed with an old friend, George Drysdale, an American businessman who generously receives many people passing through his area. Debi, Brian, and Mia also stayed with them for two nights.

While in Manila our whole family stayed two nights at the luxurious Manila Peninsula Hotel. We enjoyed elaborate breakfast buffets like I had never seen. Little Mia was just 17 months old and truly the life of the party. She enjoyed the water fountains the most.

We hired a van with driver to take us around each day to see the sights. The van actually only had seats for nine, but all sixteen of us squeezed in; no seatbelts in this country. But no traffic moves very fast, so the accidents that do happen are usually only fender benders. We included Corregidor Island in our tour, as well as Rizal Park, Manila Hotel (where McArthur had his headquarters during WWII), the Intramurals area (the oldest district of the city of Manila), and the site where Filipino hero Jose Rizal was executed by the Spanish.

In the van, Mia would get passed from the front to the back, bringing joy to everyone on whose lap she sat. As we traveled in the van, it was fun watching the family members who had never been in the Philippines before (Brian, Tony, Brittney, Dominique, Grandpa Dick, and Robin) experience life on the street and the congested traffic. Cars, bicycles, pedi-cabs all vie for the limited space — without lines — so whoever gets there first gets through the traffic. We had lived with this for 32 years, but we also had been gone from it for 18, so I often had to close my eyes so as to not "freak out."

We visited Faith Academy, where all the children had attended school. It was fun to see how it has developed, and through the generosity of a Korean Christian businessman, they now had an Olympic-size swimming pool, a beautiful theater, and a science building. God always blesses what He possesses.

We also stopped on the way to see how one missionary is helping the poor by providing a clean place for giving birth to their babies. They get lots of TLC from the Christian staff.

It was a joy for all of us to be able to attend the Christmas Eve Service at Union Church, where Fred served as associate pastor from 1985-1991. Afterwards we were invited to the lovely home of The Tornos who came to Christ under our ministry 25 years ago.

On Christmas Day we drove up in the mountains to the Taal Volcano. This is the only volcano in the Philippines that is surrounded by water. We took small speed boats over to the volcanic island, where each one of us got on a small horse. I particularly remember how funny David looked, with his long legs almost touching the ground when he got on the horse. Debi couldn't go because of Mia, so we just enjoyed hanging out together for a couple of hours while the others rode up to the volcano. Then we returned to the mainland. We were supposed to have lunch with Fred's old friend, Don Gauldin; because of traffic we just couldn't get there, so we decided to head back to Manila. We ended up having Christmas lunch at McDonald's! But back at the Manila Penn, we enjoyed a scrumptious dinner together, except for Debi and Brian, who didn't get the message in time.

The next morning we left the hotel for the final leg of our journey — Boracay Island. Only David and Lyndi had been there before with her parents, and they spoke so highly of it that we just had to go. Getting there, however, was quite a challenge — flying to another island, taking a boat to another island, and then traveling two hours by van to the beach. We were all very happy when we finally arrived at this lovely resort, just a stone's throw from the beach. What a wonderful four days we had there!

Each morning, we met for breakfast on the shaded veranda and enjoyed a buffet with almost anything one could want. The first morning, I decided to introduce 17-month-old Mia to each member of this big family. I took her by the hand, and as we stopped at each person at the table, I would tell her his or her name. When I had finished with our family, she wanted to go on to the next table and have me introduce her to all the other people at the resort! That's when I realized that she was a real flutter-bug. Today, at four years old, she loves to meet new people.

The beach was so relaxing and beautiful with all the white sand. Little shops and restaurants of every kind lined the beach. We enjoyed such a variety of foods each day, trying a new place to eat each evening. We girls all enjoyed shopping as well, and brought home many gems for ourselves and for those of the family who were not able to go.

Soon it was time to pack up and head for home with all our great memories, pictures, and gifts. More than sightseeing in each of our journeys, I believe I most enjoyed traveling with family and meeting people of various cultures. Isn't that what makes the world beautiful?

Chapter 20

FRESH WINDS
"Worship is our response to God's Extravagant Grace"

Though we had enjoyed our six years at the Bible Fellowship Church, we longed for more intimate expression in our worship. Since we joined the Vineyard in 1981, we felt it was time to reestablish our connection with them. So we joined the Inland Vineyard Christian Fellowship Church in Corona. Some of our closest friends from our former church had already started going there and encouraged us to come. We found a wonderful fellowship more in line with our beliefs and our passion. The format at the Vineyard church was quite different than other churches we had attended. Their top four values are:

Worship Word Wonder Walk

Every event starts with about a half-hour of songs that truly worship the Lord. On Sunday mornings, after this time of free style expression of Worship, we are silent and wait to hear if God wants to speak to us. Often people approved by the leadership will give messages of what they sense God might be saying to us. These are in agreement with 1 Corinthians 14:3 - - these words must be given to edify, to encourage, or to instruct. Sometimes people will see "pictures" or visions and give those; then they will be interpreted as to their meaning to the Body.

The sermons are always about God speaking through his Word to our hearts. After the message, people are invited to come to the front and receive prayer for various needs they have. Some have been convicted by the message and want to repent; others want prayer for physical or personal needs. Each person, usually among about 10 or 20 people, gets prayed for by members of the prayer team. It is such a joy to see people set free from sin and guilt; we see God changing lives weekly.

All praise to His Name!

Recently I went to the altar for prayer and waited for someone to come and pray for me. The sermon had been about "God being enough"; I wanted prayer to help me overcome my perfectionist tendencies. Two of our most anointed pray-ers came to pray for me. As they prayed, one had a picture of a huge shield of faith covering me with a hole in it; she explained that I had great faith, but that there was a hole in my shield right where my heart was. I burst into tears. Then the ladies prayed for God to heal that hole. This is the way people are ministered to and brought to freedom and healing.

One Sunday morning, a lady (whom I will call Ann) raised her hand after the service to receive Christ into her life as her Savior and Lord. I was asked to pray with her. She confessed the sin of embezzling funds from a company, and now she had been caught. She was very repentant! God certainly was using this in her life to get her attention.

This began a discipleship relationship with her until now. It was so amazing to see God work in her life and teach her how to Walk with Him. Our church surrounded her with love and prayer, not judgment. Sometimes as many as 10 people would show up early in the mornings at the courthouse when Ann had to appear before the judge. We would all pray together before she went in. One of the men in the prayer group, a friend of the husband of this lady, was a Muslim who later became a believer in Christ because he saw the love and support given to Ann.

Very often the court would postpone the trial for one reason or another; I believe God allowed this so Ann could get more grounded in the Lord before she had to go to prison. But one day she said to me, "Ruth, I feel the Lord told me this morning that I would be taken into prison today." She was right; what blessed me is that she had really learned to listen to God speak to her.

For 10 months I would go with her husband, and sometimes with Fred, to visit her in prison. She began to pray for the girls in prison. The girls at the prison made a special table where only those who wanted to know more about God would sit. Ann would talk with them and read the Bible to them. (She really needs to write her own story, as it is really quite fascinating.) Ten months later she was sentenced; the accusing party lawyer was trying to get her sentence to be nine years. About 14 of us were with her in the courtroom praying. What joy we experienced when the judge ruled that the time she had already served was enough. Of course, she had to pay back twice the amount she had stolen, but she was set free that day! We were all so stunned that we just sat there until it sunk in. God had truly answered our prayers! There was great rejoicing that day!

While Ann was incarcerated, she personally shared the Lord with many of the girls. When I would visit her, she would tell me about them and I would pray for them. When they were released from prison, I would meet them and try to help them get on their feet again. They almost always went back to their old lifestyles, except for Cory. Let me tell you her story.

Cory was doing drugs with a boyfriend in his truck with a gang of others at a ranch. Cory's boyfriend went to find food, and was gone for about two weeks. Cory and her dog were living in the truck. When she took the last of the drugs, she realized she had taken too many and began crying out, "Somebody help me!" Then she passed out. About fifteen minutes later, the police surrounded the camp. Everyone else had fled, and the police found Cory alone in the truck and got medical help for her. She ended up in the same jail as Ann. Ann reached out to her telling her about the true love of God. Cory had never been taught about God and she quickly and wholeheartedly embraced the "Lover" of her soul. Ann and Cory became very close friends in jail as Ann continued to teach Cory about God. When she got out of jail, she called me and I went down and got her. She had no clothes, no food, and no money. She did have a place to stay -- in a sober living house in downtown Riverside.

Since I had been fooled a number of times before, I wasn't sure I could trust her, but I just prayed for God to give me wisdom. First I took her to a thrift shop, and gave her $20 to go in by herself and get some basic clothes. Next I took her to the 99-cent store and gave her another $20 so she could get some basic foods and fresh veggies and fruits.

This held her over until she could begin to get food stamps. She entered a government- run program called ROC. This was a very strict program, and if students were caught back on drugs, they went back to jail. Cory finished the one-year program and graduated. She also got involved with AA. She is still very active in AA and is now sponsoring another girl.

I came alongside her as a friend and spiritual mentor. My joy was seeing her grow in the Lord. I remember how she would weep each Sunday in church as she experienced God's love for her. She was so grateful to God for rescuing her from her deeply sinful life. God heard her cry for help, even though she didn't know enough to even call His Name!

On the day of her baptism, 10 of her former friends were there to witness it. Unbeknown to me she had sent out invitations to them to come! Perhaps we should follow her example in our churches. There they were, all 10 of them dressed in black, and covered with tattoos and jewelry.

Life was tough for her, but she kept plugging along, making amends with all her children, her mother, and her sisters. It's been so great to be a part of her life and watch God care for her. Eventually she got a job as a dog groomer -- a skill she already had. The supervisor saw her potential and promoted her to manager. At AA, she met a wonderful man, Mark, who is a very strong Christian. I had the privilege to be her maid of honor at a beautiful outdoor wedding on September 4, 2010. Most recently she has been promoted to store manager. Her testimony shines brightly in her workplace, and God's favor is upon her.

A few months ago she gave her story at our Women's event. She has spoken many times at AA, and also gave her testimony to the seven judges in Riverside as an example of how effective their ROC program was. As she spoke, she gave credit to God, who changed her from the inside out.

There are many more stories that I have from my experience in mentoring women, but I just want to tell you one more. Candy came into my life at our former church when she was just 30 years old. She had just rededicated her life to the Lord and asked me to disciple her. She was married and had two teenage stepchildren. Since this has always been the joy of my heart, to help others grow in their love and devotion to Jesus Christ, I replied with a hearty "YES!"

As I've seen her go through the "valley of the shadow of death" a few times, I am so thankful that I could often be there to pray for her and to just give her the love she needed at the moment, as well as teach her how to experience more of Jesus in her life. As she grew in the Lord she learned to hear His voice and obey it — not all the time, but when she fell He would pick her up again, hold her close, and tell her to just rest in Him. She received what we refer to as the Baptism of the Holy Spirit when she was about 35 years old, and began to experience a deeper love for the Lord and a hunger for more of His Word. Soon she was also teaching God's Word.

Candy told me recently that the greatest gift I gave her was unconditional love. She said she always felt she could tell me anything because she knew I would not judge her, no matter what her problem was.

What a joy it was 10 years after this that she and her husband moved into the condo attached to ours — right next door! What a blessing it is to have a spiritual daughter of kindred spirit so close! They moved in just weeks before I was diagnosed with osteomyelitis and had to have antibiotics given intravenously. This was a line about 20 inches long that had to be inserted in my arm and went to the heart. It could take as long as five hours a day to complete the process. Her husband, Kirk, is a nurse, and a couple of times we called him in emergency situations; he was so willing to come over and help. Fred, however, learned how to attach and detach the picc line twice a day. He was extremely careful to follow about 10 steps in this procedure. I am so grateful for his loving care. He took care of not only me, but also the housework and cooking. He is a fabulous husband; every woman needs one like him.

In 2004, Fred was considering retiring from BGEA. After reading the Bible story of Caleb asking God at the age of 85 for "one more mountain," Fred prayed for that also. God soon answered that prayer when we were invited to attend the Vineyard Mission's Conference that year. One of our speakers was a man from Indonesia who was head of the YWAM mission and had started over 17 orphanages. He and his wife were currently running an orphanage of 160 children in East Jakarta. Loudy's passion was to develop Vineyard churches in Indonesia. This sparked a passion in Fred to help in this venture. This has been his "one more mountain."

The Vineyard church we were attending was very good at reaching out to the poor, but beyond outreach to Mexico, they had done almost nothing in foreign missions. However, one team had gone to Africa shortly before we joined the church.

Fred hopped on board and has been very active in this ministry since 2005. He took a team of 17 young people and adults to Indonesia for the first time in 2006. This has been a great passion for him; he has set up a screening and training program for those who would be going. A team-training ministry is now ably handled by others. Fred also has built strong friendships with our Indonesia partners in ministry. We are so thankful for many people who have helped send him there on his many trips, including Kevin and Robin, and David and Lyndi. He also helped set up the training schools for pastors; presently he is on the curriculum development team for these schools.

170

The method of training after the initial month is to send the students out for four months to minister in the villages; then they come back to the center for another three weeks for training. This continues for one year. So far over 100 students have finished their training, and more than 30 are committed to some type of outreach. Most of the rest are involved in local church plants.

For the past 6 years, Fred has taken at least 15 trips to Indonesia, and at this writing is still active in this ministry.

About 30 years ago, I felt the Lord speak to me from Titus 2:4, which says, "Encourage the young women to love their husbands, to love their children, to be sensible, pure, workers at home, kind..." I took these words as a mandate to me and began mentoring women in the Philippines, which I have been doing ever since. This has been my passion in life -- to help women know who they are and why they are here on this earth. Ann, Cory, and Candy are just a few examples. They have taught me so much as we have walked together through troubled waters. Sometimes I am at a loss as to how to help or not help, but my goal is always to teach them to pray and seek to the Lord for answers. As I pray for them, often the Lord will give me ideas on how to encourage them.

Since we moved to Park Granada in 2000, God has opened up so many unusual opportunities for me to share His love. I soon found others in this community eager to study God's Word, so I started teaching a weekly Bible Study. Let me just tell one amazing story that happened with the first group of ladies who attended.

About six women began studying on the subject, "Who is Jesus?" We would take turns answering the questions in the study guide by first reading the Scriptures. One day after about three lessons, it was Kiersten's turn to answer the question; as she read the Scriptures aloud she suddenly stopped, looked up, and said, "That means I'm living in sin." Another girl in the group joined her by saying, "If you are living in sin, then so am I." The Holy Spirit was convicting them through the Scriptures that having an intimate live-in relationship with someone without being married was sin. Both of them accepted Jesus into their lives that day and soon got married. That was about eight years ago, and they are still together with their spouses. The Word of God is powerful! (Hebrews 4:12)

During the summer of 2000, I met a Jewish couple at the swimming pool, Lucy and Aaron. They both had barely escaped from Hitler's slaughter of the Jews in 1938 and immigrated to the USA. I enjoyed learning so much about their experiences and their culture. This began a wonderful friendship for the next eight years.

I had many opportunities to share with them about the Messiah. I even bought a Jewish Bible and began taking the Bible to the pool and reading to them from it, showing them from the Scriptures the prophecies about the Messiah that were fulfilled in Yeshua (Jesus). After Aaron passed away, Lucy asked to see Mel Gibson's movie, "The Passion of Christ." As we watched it together with my friend, Sharon, Lucy kept asking questions. At the end of the movie, she very angrily said, "I can't understand why God would make His son suffer like that!" I said, "Lucy, that's what it's all about." Then I explained to her why Jesus died – He became the sacrificial Lamb for our sins, once for all time.

It was about this time that Lucy asked me if I would like to become a member of the Jewish Senior Club at her Temple, basically so I could get a discount on the day tours we often took together. Of course I joined. We met once a month for a potluck luncheon and program. After the very first luncheon, as Lucy and I were leaving, one of the ladies asked, "So are you going to convert?" I said, "No, but since we are all God's people I thought it would be great if we could get to know and just love one another." However, a year later a mandate came from the Jewish head office in Los Angeles that no non-Jew could be a member of the Jewish club. Lucy said I could still come with her to special events, which I did, and I was always warmly welcomed. I had many opportunities to share stories

172

about my life, and the leader would even call on me to share; I felt that this lovely group of people had really accepted me.

I would occasionally go with Lucy to the temple for worship, so one day I asked her if she would like to visit our Vineyard church. She came the very next Sunday. I explained to her some things that would be different than she had in her Temple worship. She was so fascinated with everything she saw that she kept telling her family and friends all about it. I feel God used that to really draw her to Himself. She died in 2008, but I believe I will see her in heaven. I told her she didn't have to join a Christian church; she could still be Jewish, but believe in her heart that Yeshua is her Messiah! My last memory of her was the day she died in her home. I held her in my arms and stroked her hair and whispered in her ear, "Yeshua loves you." She turned and said to me, "Ruth, it's you!" She died a few hours later.

After Lucy passed away in 2008, I was invited to take her place playing Mahjong with the Jewish ladies in the neighborhood. They told me that Lucy often talked about me. I often wonder what she told them. I am really enjoying getting to know these ladies. Occasionally, I even win at Mahjong. But I still miss Lucy; she came into my life just about the time my mother died, and I prayed that God would give me a mother. I didn't get just any mother — I got a Jewish mother — the best kind.

I would like to close this book with something that has helped me live my life purposefully. Years ago, I taught a 10-week series of classes based on the book, "Experiencing God" by Henry Blackaby. I have tried to practice these seven principles in my daily life since that time. I feel they have helped me live a very enjoyable, freeing, and fulfilling life in such a way that honors our God; perhaps the reader of these memoirs might also find them helpful.

1. God is always at work around you. Look expectantly for Him.

2. God pursues a continuing love relationship with you that is real and personal.
3. God invites you to become involved with Him in His work.
4. God speaks by the Holy Spirit through the Bible, prayer, circumstances, and the church to reveal Himself, His purposes, and His ways.
5. God's invitation for you to work *with* Him always leads you to a crisis of belief that requires faith and action.
6. You must make major adjustments in your life to join God in what He is doing.
7. You come to know God by experience as you obey Him and as He accomplishes His work through you.

Missions is not a place -- it is a lifestyle.

And to me, that's what life is all about!

EPILOGUE

Certainly, not everything that happened in my life has been written in these pages. But these accounts are written so that the reader might see the Hand of God leading, guiding, protecting, and blessing His precious child -- me.

I trust that you have also seen how God has worked in my personal life. I know that I am still a "work in progress," but I also know that without God I would be very lost in this dark world.

He, the Potter, knew me even before I was conceived in adverse circumstances. He was there through the many illnesses I faced, and each time He healed me. He was there when I was molested. He was there when I lost my first baby. He was there through my pain and sorrow, and He only allowed those things into my life that would mold me into the person He wanted me to be. Because of His hand of love and His healing, I am becoming whole and free.

My experiences of healing have helped me grow more and more in love with God. Therefore, I have been able to come alongside women who are going through difficulties in their lives. This has been a great joy to me, not that I have done much other than just love them and point them to God. And what delights me so much is seeing God work in their lives, changing them just like He is changing me.

What joy there is partnering with God in this needy world to:

Bring Good News to the afflicted;
Bind up the brokenhearted,
Proclaim freedom to the captives,
To comfort all who mourn.

Giving them a beauty instead of ashes,
The oil of gladness instead of mourning,
The mantle of praise instead of a spirit of heaviness

So they will be called Oaks of righteousness—
The planting of the Lord, that He may be glorified! (Isaiah 61)

"All praise and glory and honor be to the only wise God, our Father."
Amen!

ANCESTRY OF RUTH LAURA JONES THOMAS

"Every person should know their roots;
the deeper the roots the stronger the tree."

FATHER'S ANCESTRY: Glenn Merton Jones. (1910-1996)

His father; **Orin W. Jones** born 1882; married Nora B. Cummins in 1904; died of Hodgkin's Disease in 1951. In later years they discovered that his death was probably caused by the toxins in paint he used daily in his work.

Orin raised seven children: two preceded him in death—a baby son and a married daughter, Blanche M. Olin. The other children are Mrs. Velma Williams, Mrs. Alnora Emmons, Glenn Merton, Eldon, and Nyle. Orin loved to write poetry so I have included one of his best:

MEMORIES OF CALVARY

Down from the ivory palaces

Into a world of sin.

Came Christ the infinite Saviour

Lost mankind to win.

He gave his life's blood on Calvary

God's only begotten son;

A thorny crown of anguish wore

But He the victory won.

177

Amazing is the love of God,

That he should for men thus die

And send His Son, His only Son,

From realms of glory upon high.

Then why reject the love of God

And Satan's will obey?

Believe His Word, accept His love

While it is yet today.

O.W.J.

A letter from Velma, his daughter, tells this about her father: "My mother and father both loved the Lord. They both had to work hard all their lives. My father worked for himself, that is he had his painting and paperhanging business. When the depression came in 1930 he lost his home. (He was only a few months from paying it off). He tried farming for awhile, but he wasn't cut out to be a farmer. His talents ran in the Arts. He sang tenor in the choir. He also took a correspondence art course art in pen and ink drawings. Bonna Bonham, 2nd oldest grandchild, lives in Gladwin, MI has some of his original drawings. He apparently saw this same talent in Glenn, his eldest son and encouraged him to also take correspondence courses in drafting."

Glenn Jones' grandfather; **Wesley Jones** (1846-1934). An interesting story about this man appeared in a local newspaper in Stanton, Mi. November 28, circa 1940:

Wesley & Almeda (Ford) Jones family

178

"Mr. Orin Jones' father, Wesley Jones had a son by his first wife. This son is the half-brother cousin of Orin Jones. Mrs. Jones died and the father married her sister, who by a previous marriage had a daughter, who became the stepsister of the first son by the marriage and before, was his cousin, being the daughter of his Aunt."

To the second marriage three children were born. Orin, Ernest, and Stella. This made Orin half-brother and cousin of his father's elder son and half-brother of his father's stepdaughter."

(I Hope the reader can follow this amusing story above)

Wesley married his first wife, Frances Artmisha Ford of Virginia in Kent County, Michigan in 1869. Two children were born to this union, Ambert and Ella. His wife died in Ionia County on the 26th day of March. His daughter Ella died at the age of eighteen months.

The second wife of Wesley was Almeda Ford (from the famous Ford family). She was born in 1844 and died March 25, 1912 at the age of 67. To this union three children were born, Estella, Orin, and Ernest. The latter died at the age of 22, August 27, 1909.

Additional information recently found in the obituary: "Mr. Wesley Jones was a member of the Wesleyan Methodist church for many years, having been converted at the age of twenty, and always taking an active part in the work of the Lord. It was his blessed privilege to do missionary work for several years in the Upper Peninsula of Michigan."

The last 20 years of his life he made his home with his son, Orin and his wife, Nora. Nora and her children took care of him until he died in 1934.

The great grandfather of Glenn was **Philip Jones** who was born about 1800. Nothing is known about his life. He probably came originally from Wales through Canada to Massachusetts and then to Michigan.

When we visited Wales in 2008 I asked an elderly lady in a card shop if she knew any Joneses. She laughed and then told me this story: "When the young men were drafted into the army in WWII, there were so many Joneses that they had to add numbers after their names."

FATHER'S MOTHER'S ANCESTRY;

Nora Cummins Jones was born 1887, died 1975.

The Cummins ancestry can be traced back to the 7th Century; the origin of the Cummins Clan in Scotland can be traced to a noble Flemish family that ruled the town of Comines. Members of that family joined William of Flanders in his conquest of England. A Robert of Comyn, leading seven hundred cavalrymen from William, seized Durham in 1069 and held it for four days. However, the townspeople rebelled and he perished in the burning of the Bishop's Palace.

When Robert the Bruce secured the throne of Scotland, the family of Cummings who were his enemies lost their land and titles. However the Cummings remained numerous in the northeast of Scotland. During the 15th and 16th centuries, the Cummings were actively engaged in public affairs. Numerous wars took place over the centuries.

In 1657, Robert Cumming of Altyre married Lucy, daughter of Sir Ludovick Gordon of Gordonstown, and when the last Sir William Gordon of Gordonstown died, Alexander Cumming of Altyre, became his heir, assumed the name and arms of Gordon of Gordonstown, and was created a baronet in 1804. His grandson, Roualeyn, became famous as a traveler and lion hunter later in the 19th Century.

A complete history of the Cummings can be obtained from THE CLANS AND TARTANS OF SCOTLAND, by Robert Bain Published by Fontana/Collins, 1985 and from THE CUMMINGS MEMORIAL, by George Mooar (Published by B.F. Cummings, 1903. The spelling of Cummings has many variations.

NORA CUMMINGS JONES - came from one branch of the Cummings clan which follows:

Isaac Cummings (1600-01-------) date of death unknown, born in Britain. In 1636 live in Essex County, MA. Records show he received a grant of 35 acres of land. By 1639 he owned a house and 150 acres. He was chosen Grand Juryman of Topsfield in 1675 and served as moderator of the Town Meeting in 1676. For many years he served as a deacon of the church in Topsfield.

Son: John Cummings (1630-1700) His first child was born in Boxford in 1657. He was taxed 10 Shillings in Rowley Village, a section of Boxford. He was listed among the commoners in 1672. In 1678-79 he served as a "gatherer" of a rate to purchase powder and bullets. His father's will left him the family 40 acre homestead. He and his wife were members of the Topsfield church from where they were sent to Dunstable to start a new church. John was chosen Selectman of Dunstable in 1982 and served for several years as town clerk.

John's Son: Abraham Cummings (1670-1706) Not much information about him except he had six sons.

Abraham's Son: Abraham Commins (1690-1755) Married Mary Richardson—had 10 children. Lived in Taunton, MA.

Abraham's Son: Stephen Coming (1736-c1810) 5 children, lived in Kent County, RI where he purchased land in 1757 and again in 1774. His son, Jacob served in the Revolutionary War

Stephen's Son: Elijah Cummings (1767-1857) 12 children; Purchased land in Niagara County, N.Y. about 1808. Federal

Censuses from 1820-1840 list him as among the "Head of Families".

Elijah's Son: Thomas Cummins (1789-1848). Probably Born in Pownal, VT. Had 8 children. Listed as "Head of Family" by Federal Census of 1820.

Thomas' Son: Horace Edson Cummins (1817-1888). He was a farmer, storekeeper, and herbal doctor, a skill he learned from members of the Tonawanda Tribe. (Mel Jones of Eagle River, Mi. has a copy of the ancient medicine book that he compiled). He moved to Michigan in 1866, settling first in Hillsdale County and then, in 1882 in Montcalm County, where he died.

Horace's Son: Simon Burdick Cummins (1845-1928) _1843_ Married Mary Alice Smith, 1869, daughter of Anson Ransom and Mary Proper Smith. They had 12 children; 4 died in infancy. He was converted to Jesus Christ at the age of 21 while in the army and lived a faithful happy Christian life. He was a charter member of the First Baptist Church of Stanton, and was always interested in God's work and did his part in helping the cause at home and abroad." (Taken from his obituary)

Horace Son Horace Edson Jr. 18 - 1950?

My father, Glenn Jones, told me that after his grandfather's wife died he sold his property and divided up the money among his children; he then took turns living with his children. They say he liked Nora's home the best so he would stay there longer than the others. My aunt Alnora, my Dad's sister, remembers taking turns fanning him with her brother, Nyle, when he was very ill. He died in 1928.

Ruth with Grandma Nora

Simon served in the Civil War as a private in Company H of the 151 Regiment of New York Volunteers from September1862-

1865. He participated in campaigns in Virginia and West Virginia and was in active combat at least four times. Due to illness, he spent four months in mid-1864 in the Division Hospital at Washington D.C. He moved to Michigan in 1866 at the age of 19 much to the disapproval of his parents. Letters written home to his parents were found many years later in an attic around 1950. Melvin Jones of Eagle River, MI, the great-grandson of Simon, has published these in a book entitled, "Give God the Glory". This volume contains a map tracing the troop movements in which Simon B. Cummins was involved; photographs of scenes from the war, and numerous photographs of family members.

Cummings Coat of Arms

*More extensive ancestry available in the files of Fred and Ruth Thomas.

ANCESTRY of GLADYS WILLIAMS JONES (mother of Ruth Laura Jones Thomas)

Father: Alfred Smith Williams (1874-1955)

First generation: The earliest record: **Robert Williams** whose descendents probably came from Wales, but moved to a more prosperous England. He was a well-to-do husbandman of West

Somerset, Norfolk, and was Churchwarden there in 1600 near the closing years of queen Elizabeth's long reign.

As a Churchwarden he was not only charged with keeping the parish accounts and responsibility for the property of the church, but also with certain definite supervision of the behavior and orthodoxy of the clergy and laity alike; his position demanded some ability and discretion. He died around 1609.

Official records also state that three Williams' brothers, Daniel, Elias, and John are listed as the "landers" at Plymouth Rock around 1620.

Second generation: Stephen Williams, his wife and son all died in the plague in 1625

Third generation: Robert Williams (1607-1693) He escaped the plague because he was a Cordwainer's apprentice at Norwich away from his home in Yarmouth where the plague killed thousands. They were Puritans and experienced religious persecution. Robert began considering following thousands of others to Massachusetts, but his wife, Elizabeth was "of good family and had been delicately reared; and when her husband desired to come to America, though a truly religious woman, she dreaded the undertaking and shrunk from the hardships to be endured. While the subject was still under discussion, she had a dream fore-shadowing that if she went to America, she would become the mother of a long line of worthy ministers of the Gospel. The dream so impressed her that she rose cheerfully and began to prepare to leave her home and kindred for the new and distant land." They arrived in Boston in 1637.

In addition to their four children, they were accompanied by two servant girls, Mary Williams, aged 18, and Anne Williams, aged 14, who may have been members of the family. They had a total of 8 children.

Fourth generation: Capt. Isaac Williams (1638-1709)

One of Isaac's sons was **Rev. William Williams** (1665-1741) married Elizabeth Cotton. He was a relative of **Rev. Jonathan Edwards** of whom it is said to have "ignited the momentous Great Awakening of the 18th century." He is mentioned many times in the biography of <u>Jonathan Edwards A Life</u> by George M. Marsden. Jonathan Edwards officiated his funeral service.

Fifth generation: Isaac Williams Jr. (1661-1739)

Sixth generation: John Williams (1689-1765)

Seventh generation: Abijah Williams (1722-1781) Served in the Revolutionary War; as a result of war wounds he died in 1781. He had 13 children. Only two survived to adulthood.

Eighth generation: Abijah Williams, Jr. (1758-1832) Abijah was a farmer and served in the Revolutionary War. He had eight children

Ninth generation: Albemarle Williams (1782-1830) He was a physician and in that capacity often made house calls to farms in the area. One source of information states. "He was killed in a horse and buggy accident coming home from a confinement case and fell asleep." He has a Masonic emblem on his tombstone. They had 10 children.

Tenth generation: Orton Williams (1810-1867) in Stockbridge, MI. Orton was a farmer but had other occupations. For several years he carried passengers, mail, and merchandise by horse-drawn vehicles, on a route between Dexter and Ionia. At one time he owned a bar in Stockbridge, MI.

The Episcopal Church established a mission church in Stockbridge about 1860 and Orton was appointed Secretary of the Vestry. When he died the Vestry selected his youngest son, Friend, to succeed him. Friend was only sixteen, and served in that position until the church was closed by the Diocese in the early 1920's. He had five children.

Eleventh generation: Friend Williams (1851-1931) He married Flora Ann Lyman. Her mother, Catharine is our Scottish ancestor. Flora was born in Gregory, MI and was cared for by my 3rd cousin, Ken Fortman, (who sent me all this information) until she died in 1921. She was Ken's grandmother.

Friend described himself as a farmer and he owned a small farm a mile west of Stockbridge. He also was a rural mail carrier. His salary was about $750 a year and his yearly pension about $720. In the official document from the Civil Service Commission of Stockbridge, MI. it mentions the appointment of Friend to this position. Friend and Flora had nine children. One of which is my, (Ruth Jones Thomas)', grandfather.

Twelfth Generation: Alfred Smith Williams (1874-1955) married Elsie Luella Bott. They had ten children; Ruby, Mary, Alfred, Wayne, Helene, Elsie, Paul, Grace and Gladys twins. Gladys was Ruth's mother. Alfred was a twin; he and his brother were born on a boat when their parents were emigrating to the U.S.

Ruth & Grandma Bott

Mother--Elsie Bott Williams (1878-1945) Elsie was born in Tollerton, England. She had two sisters and one brother. One sister was Mary who married an architect from Chicago and lived there most of her life. She had no children. Rachel married a Catholic and was disowned by the family. The brother, Thomas Smith, served in the Civil War and was a prisoner at Chanceforsville. He died after the war of his wounds.

Her father-in-law and his brother, Edmund came to Michigan and homesteaded in Munith. Edmund had a red mustache; this reddish hair distinction can be seen in a number of the children. Uncle Ed was very skilled with his carving knife and made many small items for the home. My Aunt Helene said she had a darning egg and a rolling pin that he made.

The parents of Elsie were: **Fredrick Bott-b1827 and Elizabeth Smith-b1831.** Elsie was the youngest of six children born 1878, 13 years after the last child. They were charter members of the United Brethren's Church where Elsie was raised. When Elsie was 16 years old she went to Chicago to visit her Aunt Mary. They took in the Chicago World's Fair in 1893. She married Alfred in 1896.

Gladys Williams married Glenn Merton Jones in 1933. Six children were born to this union: Ruth, 1934; Wesley (Bud), 1938; Gerald, 1943; Nathan 1945; Karen, 1950; Lois, 1954.

I will close this ancestry lineage with a very interesting story:

The Queen of England, **Mary Elizabeth**, gave a set of 12 demitasse tea spoons to her "Mistress of the Queens Tea", Mary Farnel , a descendant of the Williams Ancestry, as a wedding gift over 230 years ago, around 1781.

These spoons have been handed down to the woman named Mary Elizabeth in each generation. At present Mary Elizabeth Waldron has the remaining four spoons. But with this gift, comes a curse, "any child named Mary Elizabeth and receives these spoons in each generation will be childless. My cousin, Mary Elizabeth was never told about this until after she had three children. She is a strong believer and follower of Jesus Christ and has the power of the Holy Spirit within her to resist such an evil omen. She did not name her only daughter Mary Elizabeth but Faith Elizabeth; perhaps the "curse" is now broken. Faith has five children! According to the story, the Queen got upset with Mary Farnel because she quit working for the Queen. According to Mary Beth, maybe she quit because the Queen had 17 children. In my files I have a copy of the letter written when the spoons were given to Mary E. Williams on August 23rd, 1911 from her great aunt Mary Sallett. They laid in her drawer for 51 years. They were given to her by her great-grandmother, Mary Farnel. I also have pictures of the four spoons.

Ruth Laura Jones Thomas (b1934) married Frederick George Thomas in 1953. They have five children:

*Daniel Kevin (b1962) married **Robin Kahn**; they have two children, **Brittney Nicole** who married **Tony Mandella** in 2008, and **Dominique Kayla (b1996)**.

* Denise Kristine (b1965) married **Craig Aamodt** in 2006.

*David Kim (b1967) married **Lyndi Parshall** in 1991; they have two children, **Ian Philip (b1995)** and **Jacqueline Rose (b1998)**.

* Daran Kris (b1969)

*Deborah Karin (b1974) married **Brian Jones** in 1999. They have two girls: **Mia Grace (b2008)** and **Zoe Kristine (b2011)**.

This ancestry section is not complete. I have the complete compilations of the ancestries in my files. I tried to give the time-line and stories that I thought would be interesting history. — Ruth Jones Thomas

Made in the USA
Monee, IL
02 March 2020

22585469R10105